The Raiment We Put On

Also by Kelly Cherry

Poetry
Beholder's Eye
Quartet for J. Robert Oppenheimer
The Life and Death of Poetry
The Retreats of Thought
Hazard and Prospect: New and Selected Poems
Rising Venus
Death and Transfiguration
God's Loud Hand
Natural Theology
Relativity: A Point of View
Lovers and Agnostics

Fiction
Temporium: Before the Beginning to After the End
Twelve Women in a Country Called America
A Kind of Dream
The Woman Who
We Can Still Be Friends
The Society of Friends
My Life and Dr. Joyce Brothers
The Lost Traveller's Dream
In the Wink of an Eye
Augusta Played
Sick and Full of Burning

Nonfiction
Girl in a Library: On Women Writers and the Writing Life
History, Passion, Freedom, Death and Hope: Prose about Poetry
Writing the World
The Exiled Heart: A Meditative Autobiography

Chapbooks/Limited Editions
Weather, poems
Physics for Poets, poems
Vectors: J. Robert Oppenheimer: The Years before the Bomb, poems
The Globe and the Brain, an essay
Welsh Table Talk, poems
An Other Woman, a poem
The Poem, an essay
Time out of Mind, poems
Benjamin John, a poem
Songs for a Soviet Composer, poems
Conversion, a story

Translation
Antigone, in Sophocles, ed. David R. Slavitt and Palmer Bovie, vol. 2
Octavia, in Seneca: The Tragedies, ed. David R. Slavitt, vol. 2

Other
A Kelly Cherry Reader

The Raiment We Put On

New & Selected Poems
2006–2018

Kelly Cherry

Press 53
Winston-Salem

Press 53, LLC
PO Box 30314
Winston-Salem, NC 27130

First Edition

Silver Concho Poetry Series
edited by Pamela Uschuk & William Pitt Root

Copyright © 2018 by Kelly Cherry

All rights reserved, including the right of reproduction in whole or in part in any form except in the case of brief quotations embodied in critical articles or reviews. For permission, contact publisher at editor@Press53.com, or at the address above.

Cover design by Claire V. Foxx and Kevin Morgan Watson

Cover art, "Affectivity," Copyright © 2014
by Dawn Surratt, used by permission of the artist.

Author photo by Burke Davis III

Library of Congress Control Number
2018955019

Printed on acid-free paper
ISBN 978-1-941209-90-5

Note from the Author

The poems herein are from *Hazard and Prospect: New and Selected Poems*; *The Retreats of Thought: Poems*; *The Life and Death of Poetry: Poems*; *Beholder's Eye: Poems*; and *Quartet for J. Robert Oppenheimer: A Poem*. All but *Beholder's Eye* were first published by Louisiana State University Press; *Beholder's Eye* was first published by Groundhog Poetry Press and is reprinted by permission. I am grateful to Rebecca Lasley for rescuing me by retyping the "Gadgetry" section of *Quartet for J. Robert Oppenheimer*.

From *Hazard and Prospect: New and Selected Poems* (2006) I decided to include only short poems. The longer poems from *Hazard and Prospect* can be found in library editions of the whole book or in used books.

Contents

Hazard and Prospect

How We Are Taken	3
The Raiment We Put On	4
Waiting for the End of Time	5
Memory	6
She Goes to War	7
Family Life in the Twentieth Century	8
The Promise	9
History	10
Death Comes to Those Who Know It	11
At a Russian Writers' Colony	12
Now the Night	13
Reading, Dreaming, Hiding	14
Woman Living Alone	15
My House	16
Grace	17
The Same Rose	18
Sunrise	19
Study for an Annunciation	20
Galilee	21
The Horse at Dusk	22
On Looking at a Yellow Wagon	23
The Shape of the Air	24
And Then	25

The Retreats of Thought

A Throw of the Dice	29
Time	30
Where Is the Past?	31
Running to Beat the Clock	32
The Special Theory of Relativity	33
A Stillness So Pure It Cannot Be Perceived	34
Matter	35
What Matters	36
That the Sense of Being Here Is Unmediated and Is a Source of the Sense of Self	37
Consciousness	38
What Is Man?	39
Self-Consciousness	40
To Descartes, on the Method	41
Deceived	42
Aspects of the Poem	43
Free Will	44
On Value	45

The Problem of Meaning	46
A Brief Review of What We Have Covered So Far	47
The Varieties of Religious Experience	48
On the Soul	49
The Problem of Pain	50
Good and Evil	51
A Theory of Everything	52

The Life and Death of Poetry

Which Is a Verb	57
A Sunday in Scotland	58
Field Notes	59
Seen but Not Heard	60
The Loveknot	61
Alphabetical	62
The First Word	63
Learning the Language	64
Talking with Only One Functional Vocal Cord	65
Against Aphasia	66
Language	67
Wintering	68
Fiction	69
Chekhov in Yalta	70
Poetic Justice	71
Ars Poetica	72

Welsh Table Talk

Welsh Song	75
On Bardsey Island	76
Rain, Early Morning, Bardsey Island	77
The Mad Friar	78
The Sheep-Fly	79
Scene	80
Welsh Table Talk	81
Line Fishing	82
The Conversation	83
Dream Daughter	84
Girls	85
A Woman in Wales	86
The Spring	87
Men Who Go to Work Each Day	88
A Day Spent Walking and Writing	89
The Manx Shearwater	90
The Last Night	91
Learning to Live with Stone	92

The Life and Death of Poetry

On Translation	95
What the Poet Wishes to Say	99
The Life and Death of Poetry	102

Gadgetry

The Virtuous Dead	109
On Not Writing a Catalogue of Ships	110
Two Not of a Kind	111
Oppenheimer and the Dean of St. Paul's Cathedral	112
New Mexico	113
Some Say	114
Newsreel	115
On Not Writing the Holocaust	116
Jews	117
Los Alamos	118
The Gadget	119
The Night He Spent with Tatlock at Her Apartment in San Francisco	120
Night	121
Despondency	122
The Teahouse at Otowi Station	123
Dido Released to the Winds	124
Dido in the Fields 0f Lamentation	125
Nights in the Secret City	126
The Office Wife	127
Omaha Beach	128
Sonnet for a B-17	129
Fdr / R.I.P.	130
An Idle Moment Some Days before the Trinity Test	131
White Sands	132
Desert Flowers	133
The Storm	134
Emily Dickinson at Trinity	135
Trinity	136
Tongues of Flame	137
Trinitite	138
Two Preludes and a Bomb	139
August 5, 1945	140
Pikadon (Flash Bomb)	141
Afterward	142
The Nature of War	143
Pity Our Myths	144
War	145

Beholder's Eye

Aesthetics	149
Art by Matisse	151
Birkenau	152
Blue River	153
In Russia	154
Crossing the Field	155
Dragonfly	156
Eclipse	157
Friendship	158

Full Moon	159
Geography	160
Helsinki	161
Indigo Bunting	162
The Jewish Cemetery in Prague	163
Krakow	164
Light on a Windowsill	165
Merida	166
Meteorology	167
The Minotaur Now	168
New Mexico Institute of Mining and Technology	169
Nostalgia of the Infinite	170
Old Age in England	171
Palm Tree	172
Parisian Skyscape	173
Question	174
Slovenia	175
Sparrow with Personality	176
Taormina	177
Tokyo	178
West to Bellingham	179
When Polar Bears Have Gone	180
Women Writers Visit the Cave of the Mounds in Wisconsin	181
Yard Art in Georgia (U.S.)	182
Xantippe	183
Zinnia	184

New Poems

Who We Are	187
Getting There	188
My Mother and Stewart Granger	190
Roses in Russia	191
Elsewhere	192
Contra Rilke	193
These Tall Trees	194
Wild Flower	195
Blossoms Dancing	196
A Writer and Her Computer	197
Husband with Book	198
War and Peace	199
Bread and Butter	200
Harriet Tubman and the Underground Railway	201
Fork and Knife	202
The Sky and the Stars	203
Author Biography	205

Hazard and Prospect

HOW WE ARE TAKEN

> Lines written while thinking of my recently
> deceased parents and what they are missing

How deeply we are taken by the world
and all its glories—how it draws us in,
until we are surrounded by the pearled
light of late day, the cool transparent rosin
of a clear sky across which the virtuoso
sun (this image reminds me of my father)
has swiftly drawn its fine Italian bow,
espressivo. And breathe—and smell—the rather
romantic, yet classical air. And feel it too—
this world's beauty present to all our senses,
surprising them, like guests who jump out at you
from behind chairs and couches, or like sentences
that draw you in and take you where you never
expected to go and wish you could live forever.

THE RAIMENT WE PUT ON

Do you remember? We were in a room
with walls as warm as anybody's breath,
and music wove us on its patterning loom,
the complicated loom of life and death.
Your hands moved over my face like small clouds.
(Rain fell into a river and sank, somewhere.)
I moved among your fingers, brushed by the small crowds
of them, feeling myself known, everywhere,
and in that desperate country so far from here,
I heard you say my name over and over,
your voice threading its way into my ear.
I will spend my days working to discover
the pattern and its meaning, what you meant,
what has been raveled and what has been rent.

WAITING FOR THE END OF TIME

Behind the window, in that room where rain
and wind were instrumentalists playing
on the windowpane, you were asleep, again,
and never heard the words that I was saying.
I didn't say them for you to hear, I said
them to your heart, that listening, third ear.

What anyone's heart knows is what has been bled
out of it. . . .

                It's February, a different year,
and spring seems something that a season might do
for the sheer delight of being sprung,
a kind of rhythm, a heartbeat, or *parlando*
(the words are spoken even though they're sung),
and everything is different now, except
time itself, which goes right on being kept.

MEMORY

These great trees, like towering sad angels,
feathery arms flung outward and down in a stasis of despair.
This stillness of spruces.
This silence.

Like death. Like the enormous absence
that is history, a chronology
that contradicts itself.

Yes, that's right. And just think of the ones you have
forgotten, the substitute teacher
in fourth grade, the friend who was briefly yours
before you betrayed her, or she you.

And the one, that man
you went walking with,
in woods outside Riga,
the green cloud of trees
in the distance, unmoving,
embalmed in memory, if remembered at all.

If not, he was never there.
You were never in that complicated country.
You never saw how the light persevered,
braving its way through massed branches of spruce, birch, and pine
to shine like a lantern, showing

the long way back.

SHE GOES TO WAR

Her face is her enemy.
She does battle in the mirror. Look!
This scar dates from Heidelberg,
that one from Saturday night.

There was a Polish boy, son of the ambassador
to Brazil, who carried a sword on the train.
All day long rain broke against the glass
and ran under the track, pooling between ties.

Back home, she lies in bed, scant sun shining
through eucalyptus leaves. Look here,
the deadliest confrontation is the one fought under cover
of camouflage, foliage

stenciled over the breast,
twigs and berries sprouting among the tangled strands
of hair she can do nothing with.
There is a man with a gun and he empties it into her chest.

FAMILY LIFE IN THE TWENTIETH CENTURY

The men go off to war
and come back with the parts of their bodies
screaming like parts of speech.
Leg! Arm! Testicle! Brain!
Their cries are like mortar fire
shelling the cities,
the turning women, restless beside them,
whose dreams are like villages
burning, burning, burning.

THE PROMISE

We thought it had been broken.
In any case, we were sick
of interminable speeches spoken
by leaders with two faces.
Let them eat feces,

we muttered to ourselves, returning
to our homes. Meanwhile, an army of clouds had begun to mass
overhead, clouds that rained fire. By the next day, our homes were burning.
Then we lived among ash and rubble.
God's face, too, we thought, was double

and death would come, despite
all assurances otherwise,
but at last we saw a kind of light,
or many lights: a rainbow. Not like the one after the flood.
A rainbow of blood.

HISTORY

It is what, to tell the truth, you sometimes feel
that you have had enough of, though of course
you do not really mean that, since you recall
it well enough to know things could be worse
and probably are going to get that way,
but still want a long and memorable life, which means
having to learn more of it day by day,
the names and dates of all the kings and queens
and those less famous who ruled the territory
known as your heart and now are gone, by one
dark route or another, from the plot of your story.
But you write on, and are your own best Gibbon,
and read on, this monumental subject being
the decline and fall of almost everything.

DEATH COMES TO THOSE WHO KNOW IT

    Lines written during the rule of the Colonels

Homer! I said, speaking to the Old One,
things are different now, the trees have thickened,
sunlight is scarcer, Greece grows cool to poets.

Sappho weeps with Alcaeus, Pindar sighs
sadly, and you avert your sightless eyes
while in the distance blind tyranny lies

over the earth like a dark cloud riven with rain.
I think truth will not shine again.
I think this chill deceitful mist had lain

in wait till democracy was done,
and now the sadder among us begin to sicken,
silence shrouds Olympus, and death comes to those who know it.

AT A RUSSIAN WRITERS' COLONY

> *Alive and burning to the end.*
> —Pasternak, "It Is Not Seemly"

In all these rooms, the Russians write
their verses, satires, monographs.
A toilet flushes. Distant dogs bark
to one another. Someone laughs—

at the satire! Another someone coughs.
They smoke too much, these Russian writers.
They hack their way through manuscripts
with cigarettes and cigarette lighters.

Their lungs are black as Stalin's moods,
as if a fire, burning the written records
of seventy years, swept through these rooms,
this crematorium of words.

Peredelkino, 1990

NOW THE NIGHT

The air loud as an imprecation
and the wind like a fist
in the face, God himself hammering
the rain in like nails,
and who won't hang on,
hang on for dear life?
Something we've done,
something we've done wrong,
the grass flattened, and rain
fleeing into the ditch
by the side of the road.
Now the brief flare of light before nightfall,
sudden as revelation.
Now the night.

READING, DREAMING, HIDING

> *You asked me what is the good of reading the Gospels in Greek.*
> —Czesław Miłosz, "Readings"

You were reading. I was dreaming
The color blue. The wind was hiding
In the trees and rain was streaming
Down the window, full of darkness.

Rain was dreaming in the trees. You
Were full of darkness. The wind was streaming
Down the window, the color blue.
I was reading and hiding.

The wind was full of darkness and rain
Was streaming in the trees and down the window.
The color blue was full of darkness, dreaming
In the wind and trees. I was reading you.

WOMAN LIVING ALONE

A book on the bed,
radio turned to a classical station.

Raining or not raining, but if it is, the water rushes
into the bushes by the side of the brick house,

bridal wreath bushes, their white flowers
like snow in spring.

If it is not raining,
there may be a blue sky like a blessing

being pronounced over a meal, which,
though taken alone,

tastes of life.

MY HOUSE

First, the hall.

On a wall in a room to the right,
a moon by Magritte hangs from a tree like a leaf.

Birds fly over the pillows.
Sunlight falls downstairs.

The study is small and scumbled with revisions.
My bedroom is not quite masterful.

All night, and the books on their shelves are leaning
toward one another in search of meaning.

GRACE

You know of course that you haven't earned it.
For if you had, it would not be what it is:
Beauty of the candle after you've burned it,
the dark bird rising like smoke, always from ashes,
remembrance of heat and light, describing itself
invisibly upon the air of the mind,
that takes the life lived in a fury of self-
love and remakes it into something that shined
so brightly that it might have been a star,
instead of the candle you were burning at both ends.
And now the night grows black, wherever you are,
except for the golden shimmer that descends
to the earth through miles of lonely outer space
and lights up your misspent life, with saving grace.

THE SAME ROSE

For so long we kept trying to
kill the divine in ourselves
with every possible instrument of destruction,
tangible and intangible,
but the divine kept resurrecting itself
quite in spite of us
(a species blind to the numinous),
so that it began to seem as if
grief and triumph were one and perennial,
petals on the same rose,
or the same rose by other names.

SUNRISE

An egret on the river's edge,
        a sky as blue as if it were
the backdrop for a Renaissance
        view of the Ascension (that slow, sure

stately flight from earthly sorrow
        into Paradise,
where angels patrol
        the hallways of God's highrise,

looking a little like egrets
        themselves, so long and white
and winged), a morning
        risen from the night.

STUDY FOR AN ANNUNCIATION

Mary in thought, though her thoughts are free of sin
even in the sinful quattrocento.
An angel's wing as wide and flat as a fin,
as if the announcing angel swam through blue
sky. This wing so richly outlandish, it could be
the glittering keel of a golden boat steered carefully
to shore, where it transformed itself into
something amphibian, whose words she heard
as if they had risen through miles of water, distant
and parsed into syllables like scuba bubbles
and saying merely what she already knew,
that even the perfect life begins below
and not on high, within the flux, the dreamy
flow that had caught her in its undertow.

GALILEE

Suppose another time while walking on water
he grew weary and decided to sit down
upon a wave cresting in a white curve
under the sun, to catch his breath, and fish
swam back and forth around him, silver needles
sewing the sea in a seamless stitchery,
the sun a sequin on the bright bodice of sky,
the anchoring hem of his robe embroidered with salt.

You on the shore! Can you imagine how
you would have felt, knowing that here was a god
at sea, one who had already gotten
his feet wet, one who, though he was not in
over his head, was drifting even then
toward the nakedness of eternity?

THE HORSE AT DUSK

He was showing himself off,
switching his tail,
thrusting his lovely head over the fence
and a bit put out when I had no sugar
to give him.
Finally, he bent one foreleg against the other
as in a bow.
Sorrel and rapeseed
sparked like the faintest of flames
in a dusk like smoke
and red poppies had ignited singly
here and there,
as if the fire were spreading.
Blue hills stood not far off,
and in the valley
the small lights of houses
came on.
Trees shook their green manes.

ON LOOKING AT A YELLOW WAGON

The yellow wagon,
motionless, in the snow-flowering field,
as a windless day,
seems to say, Whatever enters
this manifold scene can become part of it, if you let it,
the way a painting of a landscape grows grassblade by grassblade,
those turbulent bushes
scribbled
or thumbprinted
into the lower-right foreground
almost, but not quite,
excessive.

THE SHAPE OF THE AIR

It was raining goldfinches.
        Pouring like water,
they filled the lawn with light
        bright as bullion.

And then they vanished,
        a stream rushing down the sky.
The light left; the coolness of their small storm left.
        We'd only memory to see them by.

Must beauty be sudden and short,
        a surprise that dies?
Or is beauty the shape of the air
        after finches fly?

AND THEN

And then a vast, surprising peacefulness
descended, like a blue shadow upon
the snow; and the shadow sleeping on the snow
was a kind of reconciliation, form
embraced by content, light by light, the birds
hanging from the branches like bright red berries.

And then for days, there was nothing to disturb
the beauty of that equilibrium,
so like the miracle of forgiveness.

The Retreats of Thought

For these philosophical questions I chose sonnets as a way
to restrict the cloudiness that might otherwise have entered in.

A THROW OF THE DICE

At any rate, I am convinced that He does not play dice.
—Albert Einstein, Letter to Max Born, 4 December 1926

The question that confronts us first is, Why
something? Why is there anything at all
instead of simply nothing, nada? I
suggest that something is more probable
than nothing—that of which there can't be more
than one at most—while on the other hand
abound glad possibilities galore
for life and stuff. Please don't misunderstand.
I can't concur with that favorite reply
of priests: "The odds against our universe
existing are so infinitely high
we must believe in God." The odds aren't worse
than for any other ordered universe.
If there's a God, He does not throw *loaded* dice.

TIME

> *From that therefore, which is not yet, through that,*
> *which hath no space, into that, which now is not.*
> —Augustine, *The Confessions*, Book XI, trans. Edward B. Pusey

Augustine thought that time unlocked the door
of the future, rushing into the present
and then the past, though it's my metaphor,
that vacated house, not his, whence went
time in such a hurry it barely brushed
the here and now, perhaps nicking a corner
or knocking off a hat that then got crushed
beneath a bus, a chill like a coroner
in its wake, a coroner with a cold,
his face as blue as any in his morgue,
where he dices some stiff whose run's been cancelled
by an untoward event that seemed as rogue
as a rogue elephant or Errol Flynn,
but no, it was time's way the dead was in.

WHERE IS THE PAST?

> *Wheresoever then is whatsoever is, it is only as present.*
> —Augustine, *The Confessions*, Book XI, trans. Edward B. Pusey

Augustine said the only time is now.
The past is merely memory, although
by memory we also mean history.
What of the past lost to the mystery
of forgetfulness, the bits and pieces
fallen like unheard trees, unthought theses,
out of mind and into nonexistence?
Suppose whole chunks have broken loose, a tense
like an asteroid belt, ranging, and out
of control, something one certainly ought
to steer around if it were there, but it
is not, is it? At least it is not quite.
Where does the time go? Ah. It goes with us
as we step to the front and off the bus.

RUNNING TO BEAT THE CLOCK

Time stretches out before us—and behind—
as far as we can see, the light of stars
a window onto time that's out of mind.
Are they the lightning bugs God trapped in jars,
fire flickering to dark? Was there a God
who wound a clock, said prayers, went to sleep,
Supreme Deity snoozing in the land of Nod?
He is not likely to be counting sheep,
which is to say, ourselves, we humans who
must run to beat the clock because the yard
Of time it measures shrinks, like sodden wool,
to next to nothing, something strayed and downward
of anything, our future and our past
both relatively brief and going fast.

THE SPECIAL THEORY OF RELATIVITY

There's no such thing as unenacted time:
time is theater, an effect whose cause
is one of physics' fundamental laws:
the body's movement is a pantomime
of point of view. You know the paradigm:
a man who's riding on a beam of light
will seem to disappear into the night—
sort of like a sentence, distracted by rhyme—
lost to his friends, for whom the years revolve
around mundane matters of love and marriage,
children, the deaths of pets and parents, work:
instead of beams of light, they know the dark
returning and returning, feel their age,
recall this life before it began to evolve.

A STILLNESS SO PURE IT CANNOT BE PERCEIVED

Begin here: space and time are relative,
and one does not exist without the other.
Thus place is what a moment has to have
to happen, and nothing happens nowhere.
Thus time is movement and eternity
stillness so pure it cannot be perceived
(as may be said also of God's pity,
unless it really is to be believed
that he so loved the world he gave to it
his only begotten son, that they should live
who him receive). Can mere mind intuit
a That to Which the way is negative?
Always, questions. I tried to clear my head
and think, but sometimes I gave up and read.

MATTER

has extension, density; can be felt:
the fall of scarf across your chilled shoulders;
the unforgiving floor on which you knelt
while weeping; dear body of love that molders
in the mute grave, despite your desperate tears.
The stars burn on like lost love, which smolders
in the heart's hearth for a while, but even stars
go out; the cosmos grows older and colder,
for substance changes form and in the process
reveals that it was never anything more
than hope and memory, the defeating farthest
distance being that which is at the core
of everything, the brute, unfathomable reaches
of space that matter, brave as soldiers, breaches.

WHAT MATTERS

What's matter but the stuff that takes up space:
a definition that will surely do
even for one who'd build an airtight case,
such as Hamlet judging his flesh too . . . too . . .
"sullied," some say, but let us say "solid,"
although, again, you know, it hardly matters.
Even the most crowded, vile, and squalid
den, compacted of addicts, outlaws, and squatters,
contains a whole unsettled, free frontier.
The body cartographs a world within,
oceans between tiny bones of the ear,
unconnected islands construed as skin,
and all that is, is so filled up with space,
we must be light and floating, fixed in place.

THAT THE SENSE OF BEING HERE IS UNMEDIATED AND IS A SOURCE OF THE SENSE OF SELF

> *"Hereness" cannot refer to a mediated web of "heres" exactly because the individual "here" is established by being out of mediated relation.*
> —Brian Martine, professor of philosophy at the University of Alabama in Huntsville, from "Where Are the Philosophers Now?"

The moment I suppose that I am here
I know I am not there—nor there—nor there,
nowhere but here, in fact, though here is there
from another point of view. Do I not hear
my heart, my greedy breaths? Come close. You'll hear
the me I am. As for the others, they're
elsewhere, and never any nearer than there.
It's so lonely being the only one here.
The world resists my charm. You might reply
that "world" includes me. Well, it does, except
when I regard it, then it's other than
myself, a thing apart. Hard though I try,
it's I who, longing for oneness, disrupt
the flow of the unmediated one.

CONSCIOUSNESS

Must consciousness be prepositional,
be "of"' some thing (however loosely "thing"
may be defined), be situational?
Or is it independent of any thing,
Platonic form the world itself might long
to emulate, as though the thought *to sing*
existed in the being of the song
you hum while thinking of everything
you meant to get right that you got so wrong?
Perhaps the music of the spheres is heard
only by those who think meaning may hang
upon the uses of a single word
like "consciousness." Or maybe not. Perhaps
celestial music is sensation and synapse.

WHAT IS MAN?

So what *are* we? Experience, I'd say.
Not *what* we experience: experience
itself. It's what we mean by "sentience,"
this being that we do every day
of our lives. Useless, Skinner, to inveigh
against the fact: it is *social* science,
with us as the irrefutable evidence
that life is feeling, how ever and any way,
but something all the time. We testify
that something happens to us. What we do
in response is not adult or child's play
but the work of living. When we die,
experience is the one thing we take to
the grave, the estate we cannot give away
(although art tries). Death is hell to pay.

SELF-CONSCIOUSNESS

I know myself as self, and furthermore,
know that this self will not persist forever,
although it seems to me it has a core
that continues like a low-grade fever
through all the hours of my shortening days,
an illness, and a diagnosable one
despite the deconstructionist who says
whatever we think we are, we are no one,
that anything we do can be undone,
including the construction of a self,
that as a writer I should know my ruin
cannot be shored against by a bookshelf,
and maybe this is true, though I'd have sworn
my self was me the second I was born.

TO DESCARTES, ON THE METHOD

> René Descartes was stationed in Neuberg, Germany, with the Bavarian army of Frederick V, when, on November 10, 1619, he envisioned a new method of doing philosophy, arguing that reason must be based on clear and distinct ideas, such as cogito ergo sum ("Je pense donc je suis"). It was Blaise Pascal who noted that "the heart has its reasons, which the mind knows not."

"I think, therefore I am," but nowadays
certain theorists might question if that "you"
is not a socially constructed Who,
linguistic figment, or hormonal phase.
"It's like putting the horse before Descartes,"
someone might say—for all I know, has said—
although anyone who's actually read
your reasoning will hear her Pascalian heart
beat harder as she thinks of you "alone
in a stove-heated room," sweeping away
all thoughts that are unclear and indistinct
(but are they only incompletely known?),
bold as a German general that day,
so ironic and Gallically succinct.

DECEIVED

> Descartes argued that because God is good we are not
> deceived in our impressions.

Epiphenomena—concomitant
but meaningless—is how some thinkers view
emotions: stuff that like a sycophant
somehow manages to latch onto you,
is always there, trying to make you feel
that you are what everything is all
about, you are both the hub and big wheel,
the world is the Response but you the Call,
it's about you, and why shouldn't it be?
You feel so much. Surely no one has ever
known such a broad array of affect so deeply,
or otherwise, our life is a fever
that consumes us, and we toss and turn,
delirious, as our deceived hearts burn.

ASPECTS OF THE POEM

> *We have defined a story as a narrative of events arranged in their time-sequence. A plot is also a narrative of events, the emphasis falling on causality.*
> —E. M. Forster, *Aspects of the Novel*

Hume proved conclusively we cannot know
if anything is caused by something else.
In other words, our narrative has no
plot, is a patched physique that lacks a pulse.
Well, *there's* a plot of sorts, and history
is buried there, the one thing coming after
another, but it's still a mystery
to me as well as to Mr. E. M. Forster
why it is that this has followed that
and not this or *that*. The novelist
cannot accept that things occur without
cause, or thinks that if they do, at least
they shouldn't in his book; wherefore, I say,
if God exists, He prefers poetry.

FREE WILL

Responsibility is the concern
here, for how can we be held liable
for actions we've not caused? It's not viable
to say that what we get we never earn;
a fact of life that each of us must learn
is that the notion of fate is a fable,
grand but flawed, or else we are not able
to make moral distinctions, say the turn

that someone did you was a good one, or
was not—and are your deeds impervious
to judgment? No. Comeuppance is a part
of being human (as, of course, is error).
And yet how fateful and how fabulous
is the irresponsible, willful heart.

ON VALUE

> The graduate philosophy department at The University of Virginia
> emphasized analytic philosophy.

In Charlottesville, at twenty-one, I was
assigned to write a paper on value:
What is value? Something that something has,
a property? Product of a point of view?
A measurement, perhaps, or function of—
what? I was working on a Ph.D.
I had long hair. We value what we love,
I thought (minutes before love became free).
My bangs fell to my eyes. I was sitting
at a small Formica table, legal pad
in hand, when it struck me I'd be quitting
school soon. I love philosophy but had,
I saw, no way within the practice of it
to say I value it because I love it.

THE PROBLEM OF MEANING

Briefly, then: I think nothing has meaning.
What is, is as it is, and yes, it has,
of course, ramifications, thus seeming
to take on grave significance in the as-
sociation with whatever else is,
although significance is not the same
as meaning, but assumes a hidden premise:
that what is meaningful is so for some-
one, meaning meaning is a kind of value,
and is that argument not circular,
making meaning what we attribute to
the meaningful, while the unblinking star
that gazes down on us without concern
observes our problematic planet turn?

A BRIEF REVIEW OF WHAT WE HAVE COVERED SO FAR

I think that something and nothing are one
thing, the moon with one side bright as joy,
the other dark, unshined on by the sun
and cold as January in Sheboy-
gan. I think creation and consciousness
are the same one side of a Moebius strip,
unending, so that each is more or less
the other. I think time is a round trip,
a journey sweet but often hard and lonely
and taken on the train of thought from here
to here, that all times happen at once, only
past, present, future are how they appear.
I think that when we die we die for good
and ever, making room in the neighborhood.

THE VARIETIES OF RELIGIOUS EXPERIENCE

To be is to become. There is no state
of being that is not provisional,
as transient as weather, spring or fall;
none not blurred, befogged, and intermediate,
or none that's actual. Plato's postulate,
a realm of forms both static and ideal,
would make the abstract realer than the real,
esteem a noun above its predicate,

and some believe in a reality
that lives forever, will be and has been,
remains with us now, and never alters,
is incorruptible, but we agree
that faith's the evidence of things not seen,

explaining the variety of altars.

ON THE SOUL

By *soul* I mean the self described by passion,
for passion shapes us. We are carved and hollowed
by what we love—love irrationally,
perhaps, and yet we think our hearts hallowed
by love that acquaints us with the contours of
ourselves, until we know ourselves as well
as the arms and legs and back and knees of love,
the body of it, sweat and salt and smell.
The love of thought is as identifying
as any other passion and survives
time's despoliation—love undying,
for as long as the sense of one's self lives,
and then the soul departs, leaving behind
the record of an open, responsive mind.

THE PROBLEM OF PAIN

Regarding the afflictions of our people
and not forgetting how the birds and beasts
suffer, under a zealous desert sun
or the whiplash winds of driving winter,
we ask how we can call creation good
that mandates loss and sorrow, that permits,
indeed, requires, of all who live, a measure
not only of felt pain, physical or
mental, but also the causing of the same
to others so that anguish must recount
its tale endlessly, like the number π,
a wife who has been left, a veteran
of a forgotten war, autistic child,
or wallpaper, the infinite blue sky.

GOOD AND EVIL

Can good and evil be defined by absence
of each other?

           Let's say that good is light
without shadow, as hard to see as night,
a sun best viewed through indirection, lens
devised to let us look up by looking down.

If evil is the lack of good, a hole
in the heart as black as a hole in space, a hell
that blinds us so we do not see our own
selves—the shadows we throw, living our lives—
it is invisible, a place we fall
into forever.

           In light of this, perhaps
we see but darkly that we might surmise
even the Absolute is not the All
for here we are, mortals in moral eclipse.

A THEORY OF EVERYTHING

No drama of dualism, nor scheme
in which the many handily resolve
to one, nor inspired poet's pipe dream
a hapless visitor from Porlock could dissolve
with a knock on the door, and not the Platonic form
of something (floating, disembodied, outside
time but imitated by a norm
that is never *videlicet* but only *vide*),
truth is existence, and existence is
itself and not-self and so it cannot hide
anywhere, while we, among existence's
thin gaps and folds, are scattered far and wide,
adrift and hidden, crying *adieu, adieu,*
as our horizon vanishes from view.

The Life and Death of Poetry

The Life and Death of Poetry (2013) offers poems about language. It begins in silence and animal sound before taking on literature, public discourse, and the particular art of poetry. The second section, a sequence titled "Welsh Table Talk," considers the unsaid, or unsayable, as a father, his daughter, his daughter's friend, and a woman spend a week on Bardsey Island off the coast of Wales. The innocence and playful chatter of the children is set next to a darker and sadder, slightly submerged—like the island itself—narrative of failed communication among the adults. In the third and final section, I consider the pluses and minuses of translation, great art's grand sublimity, and the divine tongue or word and its relation to an everyday, secular world.

WHICH IS A VERB

We fell out of eternity
into time, which is a verb.
Life was rushing past us,
and we began to rush too.
Everything was a blur. In the confusion,
some things got mixed up with others.
A loaf of bread drove a bus.
A longleaf pine swam in the pond.

We grew so dizzy, light sparked
beneath our closed eyelids, like rescue flares.
We lay down on the red grass
and clung to the world as it whirled.

Wind whistled past our ears.
Tears flew from our eyes.

A SUNDAY IN SCOTLAND

I found a path that led me through the wood,
past fallen stone—a Roman wall in ruin—
and some felled trees, to where two horses stood
at pasture, and the nearest, a graceful roan,
drew close, and backed away again, and then
came partway back, and then decided to get on
with his own life in that field next to a fen.
I found a stump nearby—something to sit on
while catching my breath. Just to my right, a field
of poppies, post-impressionistically
spattered. The sky was gray. The church bells pealed,
and I was thinking how it would be, to be
on earth as horse or dog or cat or bird
or tree or flower, self-consciousness deferred.

FIELD NOTES

Death underfoot wherever you walk,
overhead, at hand.

The bird flat on its back,
the shrew, its face sharp as a pencil.

And the bee silent upon the sill.

The spider whose web goes on snagging flies for dinner
even after she's been bagged and eaten.

A shrew is so small,
it is amazing that it lives at all,

with a tail as long as a tirade.

SEEN BUT NOT HEARD

A thrill of cobwebs in the trees,
the breeze strumming gossamer like a guitar.
What's to be done about these bright notes,
this unuttered air?

There must be a melody
heard only by the bees
and flies who die
to hear its harmonies,

a melody like none other,
accomplished and uncanny.
O these night notes,
these undertones, these useless prayers

no human hears.

Night returns to day.
Cobwebs tremble in lighted air.
Beeches catch the sun
and toss it back like a ball,

and trapped things pray
sotto voce.

THE LOVEKNOT

On the couch—
baby mice stillborn,
would-be twins
clutching each other
as if either
could save his brother.

The size of thumbs,
tails still curled.

Two Q's
spelling nothing.

Spelling it twice.

ALPHABETICAL

Breath of wind that clouds the moon.
Shriek of eagle, cry of loon

threading through fog.
The throaty frog.

Death-scream of a mouse
the roaming cat returns with and proffers on the stoop.

And is that you I hear, weeping
while the rest are sleeping?

O, O, O, O, O
u, u, u.

THE FIRST WORD

Someone said it. Maybe
a child calling for his mother.
Maybe a lover, inventing
the word *you*. Maybe
a hunter giving his clan
the signal to kill.

Was there delight on the mother's face?
Did the beloved preen in the mirror of her lover?
And the beast, alarmed
by the human swarm
around him—did he hear
the tribesman's command
and know that it was the last word?

LEARNING THE LANGUAGE

> Alex, African grey parrot, 1976-2007

Before he had the word for it
he must have apprehended the thing itself:
its raptures, obligations,
that it supported his right to exist.

He knew the cool warmth
of her unfeathered skin
beneath his claws, saw
how she smiled broadly when
his wings grazed her bare arm,
his black bill nudged her hand
resting on the arm of the chair,
he flew from his perch to her nape.

Or did he put on knowledge
with her caress, her constant coo
and call?
        She gave him
a lexicon for life in the lab
a way to speak his world
and if *love* was a word
it had to mean
something, meant what mattered most.

And so he responded, convinced
by her mouth and human throat
shaping sound: *red, green, yellow,*
more, none, same, different, other, banana, kiss.

He had thought they were singing a duet
and that they would go on singing forever.
Good night, he told her, that last night.
I love you, he said.
See you in the morning.

TALKING WITH ONLY ONE FUNCTIONAL VOCAL CORD

It's work to push the syllables out,
and sometimes they stick inside
like children refusing to go outside
to play, and then I have to shout

though what comes out is a whisper,
a kid too shy to make friends
on the playground, who pretends
to like being alone. I have a sister

who played the flute at Wigmore Hall,
her fingering fluent as a goldfinch in flight.
I think of her late at night
when speech stops and the silenced call.

AGAINST APHASIA

1.
The words have flown
sprouted wings and taken off

Your throat is an empty nest

Come back, you want to cry,
but you can't—

You learn to write.
It's the only way.

2.
One day birds line up
on a branch of the cedar

to take their turns at the feeder.

You name them chickadee, bunting, wren—

words you can't say
but still believe in

3.
So you write
and words line up on the ruled page
like birds on a branch
and sing to you

the sparrow his spunk
the robin, matins
the bluebird his happiness

You feel like crowing.

LANGUAGE

Conceals and discloses.
Lies and belies.
Discourses on roses
("A rose is a rose is . . .").
May be a disguise.

May invoke a muse.
Or obfuscate.
You choose:
Purple prose?
Boilerplate?

Language is a sorcerer
and may so entrance
the dedicated listener
she cannot tell the dancer from the dance
or syntax from the sense.

And it may ennoble
the soul, electrify the mind,
beautify the Chernobyls
of our devastated hearts, and enable
us to know our human kind.

WINTERING

The asparagus, the ivy, and the anonymous
summer vines, unleafed, snarled in snow,
lean against the wire dog-pen.
The wind is from River Falls,
and before that, Idaho. My house is lighted
against the dark. On their shelves, books

huddle in their jackets. I have read the books
that tell of difficult journeys and anonymous
desires, of lanterns that have lighted
the way to Arcadia or the North Pole, books that explain snow,
or the way living things grow, or the way lovers fall
in love, each to the other an open

book, as if love were the pen
writing, and their lives a book.
I stand looking out as the snow falls
obsessively. The night is anonymous.
Supper will be snow
baked in the oven I have lighted,

birch bark, roots, and berries, dressed with light,
served on a paper plate with a pen
for a fork—a low-calorie diet, light as a single snow-
flake, not found in cookbooks
but typical of anonymous
readers en route from Wisconsin to Borneo or Victoria Falls.

While I eat, I read and the snow falls
on the tangled vines too light-
weight to stand up to snow. Anonymous
as a nun, I write books, pushing my pen
across paper, or read others' books,
in a room as quiet as falling snow.

It's no
secret that one who reads can occasionally fall
to thinking how life in books
is so much more exciting and enlightening
than her real life, in which she's penned
up, isolate, and anonymous.

*The snow falls
lightly as starlight* is the sort of thing one reads in books
penned by Anon.

FICTION

It has a plot,
or, fashionably, not.

Characters live
and die, mostly
the ones we love.

The setting
is where the characters live
and die. A modern executive
does not often live or die
in rural Mississippi.

In a novel, dialogue need not be so concise
as in a short story and may continue
for hundreds of pages,
which we will turn if what is said
is interesting enough.

Is Monsieur short and squat?
Does Madame wear a hat?
Would Mademoiselle enjoy
a ladyfinger?

There may be symbols, too.
That ladyfinger *means* something.

At last the theme
reveals itself, taking
it all off under the hot lights,
the cool gaze,
the critical view.

CHEKHOV IN YALTA

Rain darkening the red squares of terraces,
    the gray stones of walkways.

Crows on a cable. And seagulls. (Of course.)

Imagine Chekhov tending to his roses,
    talking to them, teasing and encouraging them.

Imagine the roses, their coy fluttering
    on the stalk as he approaches.

And after he goes back into the house,
    what they say among themselves.

Their rustling skirts, the susurrant sighs.
    Black Sea blue against blue skies.

Him at his desk, jacket off,
    proceeding to revise.

POETIC JUSTICE

> *The quality of mercy is not strain'd.*
> *It droppeth like the gentle rain from heaven.*
> —William Shakespeare, *The Merchant of Venice*, Act 4, Scene 1

Not from the poet—
from somewhere—where?—
the poem acquires

the quality of mercy,

reviving us
as does the gentle rain
green leaves;

it is not strain'd

but touches us all,
a miracle
like the loaves and fish,

that democratic dish.

In dark times,
when the city is discouraged
by its own malfeasance

or difficult circumstance,

the poem instructs us
in responsibility.
When we are alone

and abject or anxious,

hiking a little-known trail
through hieroglyphic woods,
the signs impossible to read

by starlight,

the poem assures us
we are forgiven,
we are but

human.

ARS POETICA

No dog, the muse cannot be leashed or trained.
The poem depends upon a *willing* muse.
Nothing is guaranteed or foreordained.

The poem is providential—a blessing gained
in bars and bordellos as often as in pews.
The poet knows the poem is not ordained.

Words upon a page are barely restrained
by form, twist like dust devils to get loose.
Nothing is guaranteed or foreordained.

Like the four winds, words will not be chained
down in stanzas merely to amuse.
The poet knows the poem is not ordained.

Even your life is not your own, feigned
as it is to please the gods—a futile ruse.
Nothing is guaranteed or foreordained.

From time to time, the mercurial muse has deigned
to breathe a poem for a poet's temporary use.
No faithful dog, the muse—nor leashed nor trained.
Nothing's guaranteed. Nothing's foreordained.

Welsh Table Talk

"Welsh Table Talk" is a section in *The Life and Death of Poetry*.

WELSH SONG

Rain blew against the window pane.
The kestrel's shadow quartered the air.
A rooster crowed. The drainpipe banged
Against stone. The child brushed her hair

And sang a song. The gas fire burned.
The gas lamp glowed. The rain fell faster.
Blue became black in the window.
The wind pulled the sea up to the pasture.

The child brushed her hair and sang songs.
The lost pigeon sheltered alone
In the chapel rafters. The red
Glass on the sill gleamed in gaslight.

A winged darkness crossed the dark night,
And the drainpipe banged against stone.

ON BARDSEY ISLAND

An island of wild wheat and long grass,
The whitewashed abbey at the foot of the mountain,
And the chough, here as if to report
Gloucester has been blinded—
That old news from the mainland.

And wind from the north shrieking its own sad cries.

The Connemara mares switch their tails,
Lift their heads to smell the wind.

Children are playing cards
On the living room floor,
And the door has swung open.

At night, the ghosts of eremites
Flicker in the mist,
Slip quickly as swifts
Through the silent abbey
Along unlighted garden paths,
Among secret coves with shallow water
And high caves.

RAIN, EARLY MORNING, BARDSEY ISLAND

The Irish Sea, secreted in mist,
Rain falling on the stone
Cottage.

No sun.
Only a silver-plated sky,
The gulls crying.

Fat sheep, invisible in fog, lying
Down, the rams with gold, sprung
Horns like flames,

As if burning,
Sacrificed to
A human yearning.

And monks who lived here
Among sea-slick rocks, on fire
With cold ideas of damnation

And penitence,
Return, almost real,
Almost incarnate,

Almost articulated
In flesh and word.

THE MAD FRIAR

The friar has gone mad.
He dances in the tower
Of the fallen ancient abbey
By candlelight in bright
Day, and a flashing wind
Lifts his gray hair
And gray beard like waves
Breaking off shore.
He dances without music
Unless he hears a music
None else hears
And his rough brown habit
Swirls around his shoes
And the sleeves spread wide
On the wind like wings,
And the rope around his waist
Is the noose he'll hang from.

THE SHEEP-FLY

You poured that very expensive
Wine, recommended, you assured us, by your vintner,
Into small kitchen glasses, making a toast.
Though evening had come ashore,
The sun was taking a long time
To set; we had already eaten.
You handed glasses to the girls, too,
Who gulped, and moved outside to play.
When I glanced again at my glass
I saw that a sheep-fly had fallen
In. How it struggled, the thin legs
Paddling, wings fluttering in white wine
As if they would be water wings.
I waited for you to offer me another glass.
Or better—more romantic—to swap
Your glass for mine. Instead,
You said, Will you allow me to get that out
For you, and reached in and cupped the now-
Dead fly in your fist.
I was expected to finish my wine, then, and you
Were annoyed with me when the best I could do
Was a few more half-hearted sips.
I had failed your test.
All kinds of possibilities were dying like flies.

SCENE

The curtain flies in the open window.
The girls are jumping on and off
The bed on which their father slept.
He has gone out in anorak
And wide-brimmed hat and Wellingtons,
And with a walking stick. The girls
Pretend that one of them is sick.
The curtain falls still, so still its shadow
Seems painted on the windowsill.
The toy penguin on the table
Has its wings spread wide. The girls
Play school and mark each other's papers.
(They have grown tired of smelling-salts,
The vapors.) He has reached the top
Of the mountain (for I can see
Him from here). The curtain stirs,
Snags on thorns and burrs. The girls
Play war and snip out pics of ships
And Spam. On an island like this,
Lacking reference points, everything
At a distance looks huge, and seen
From the crown of the furze-covered mountain,
A rooster will look as big as a man.
The girls bring tea to the toy penguin.
The freed curtain flies in the open
Window, and the jam-jar daisies
That were picked from the garden spill
On the floor like girls galore.

WELSH TABLE TALK

There is a dragon in the garden,
The first one says. *Papá*, says the second,
Seated cheerfully on the rescued church pew,
Bronwen has put her cold mittens

To my leg. The dragon in the garden
Is quite a nice dragon, says *Papá*.
The second one says, Nasty Bronwen
Has put her cold mittens to my ears.

The first one says, The dragon is eating
All the mulberries, and the roses
As well. *Papá* shakes his bald head
And says, I never cared for roses

Myself. The second one squeals, Bronwen,
Stop it! The first one says, The dragon
Is eating the garden and there won't be any
Garden left. *Papá* likes Marmite

And margarine on his toast, and seventeen
Cups of tea a day. The first one says,
How sad it is that our garden is gone.
The second asks Bronwen to come out and play.

LINE FISHING

Papá and daughter fish in shape-shifting pools
That lurk among the sheared-off rocks.
Their lines play out from hand-held spools.
But then: "I'm bored," she says and breaks

For freedom. Oh Gwynnie's gone
To look for her young friend,
The golden doe-eyed fawn
Named Bronwen.

Papá and I avoid each other's gaze:
He's focusing on fish.

Before the sun's burned off the morning haze
We've thought each other selfish.

The voices of the girls carry from the chapel
A cappella.

THE CONVERSATION

She has found a snail
And lets it travel her arm.
Look, she says. Isn't it sweet?

(I think she is sweet,
Wonder if she's my stepdaughter-to-be.)

The eyes sentinel atop two small stalks
Like periscopes.

Its face is blank as wax,
Translucent, the shell
A sand-and-cream swirl,
A kind of mint.

She waits patiently
While the snail traverses her arm,

Which is brown with summer,
Smooth as a snail's shell.

We have so far to go.
We have come this far.

DREAM DAUGHTER

I heard you singing
In the chapel,
Pedaling the tired piano,

Crashing chords with abandon.
I saw you washing your hair
In holy water,

Saw you braiding your hair
As you walked on the mountainside,
Wind gently slapping the thrift

Back and forth,
Fennel and thyme
Sheltering beneath blue mallow.

Your hair, sun-dried and set
Loose, tumbled and fanned
Out in waves. The sea waved back.

The white duck with red markings
Around its eyes
Rolled from side to side like a sailor

As it crossed the grass.
Later, in the garden,
Where the mallow was,

By moonlight
I saw you setting tea-things on a table,
And the wind snapped the tea towel

Smartly, and the brass
Kettle you were holding by the handle
Shone, a star.

GIRLS

They go off somewhere
Where they can't be found,
And there they paint the sun
In watercolor, write
Poems about horses.

Or else they sit stubbornly in rain,
A plastic sheet over their heads,
Wanting to know how it feels to be homeless.

Wildflowers and flowering weeds blossom in their hair,
Bracelet small wrists.

There is such a power here,
It could turn the earth on its axis.

The shy, smiling girl.
The bold girl in blue jeans who twists on the couch,
Crossed legs over her head—
She rolls her eyes,
Tries on accents,
Acts.

All day, and they are at the lighthouse
The bird observatory
The ruined abbey.

One day you come across an old album, discover
A faded watercolor,
A poem that rhymes *horse*
With *gorse*.

A WOMAN IN WALES

A woman in Wales
Shares a cottage by the sea.
Wind fills and luffs her hair like sails,

Dispatches clouds cross country,
Sending rain. In the sky, a light opens—
Then closes as if locked by latchkey.

Indoors, she puts away her notes, pad, and pens,
Fixes herself a cup of hot chocolate,
As women do in kitchens

Almost anywhere, but here, on a late
Afternoon in Wales,
The sea is as blank as if God would uncreate

Creation, no boats now or fishermen, only gales
Of steam climbing from her cup, a slick lacquer of cream
Cooling the chocolate, not even the mails

From the mainland running. Around here somewhere,
A newly abandoned dream, but what is a dream
But something that was never there?

THE SPRING

We went for walks but not together.

My footpath led me past meadow rue
Around a bend at the base of a hill
Where sprites were gathered, and there

I found a spring, almost invisible
But loud as a song
Three tenors might sing.

The water slipped over cool shale
Into a field where the children were having
A make-believe Bake Sale.

Tuppence for a mud pie, a shilling for a roll,
A bun's a farthing. Sir, are you on the dole?

I drowned a penny in spring water,
Wishing for a daughter.

MEN WHO GO TO WORK EACH DAY

And morning after morning they put on
The uniform of work—policemen, letter
Carriers, mechanics, waiters, well-built construction
Workers in yellow hard hats . . . do it whether
They wish to or not, these unknown men, with bosses
Who rule from nine to five like little tyrants
And add up everything in terms of losses
And think employees should be sycophants.
The teacher, the teller, even the NCO
Has someone over him, drawing a line
Somewhere, that he has always got to toe.
I think these men are sturdy, true and fine,
Arriving home at dusk to change their clothes,
Become the husbands and fathers everyone knows.

A DAY SPENT WALKING AND WRITING

She stepped mindfully
Around the sheep dip,
The long slugs sliming
In dew, the snails.

Soon the sun was up,
And a fresh wind filled the sails
Of the boat, so far out it seemed to be miming
Progress rather than really

Making any, but she had covered miles,
And now the island was wholly
Dark, clouds worn thin as slippers.

Another day gone to pacing and rhyming.

THE MANX SHEARWATER

On nights when there's no moon, the Manx shearwater
Will cry—almost a howl, a dog baying
At the moon, but no moon rises over water
And night is black beyond any mere graying.
Scientists study what these birds are saying;
The locals feel that it's a simple matter
Of socializing, of getting it on—and laying
Some eggs, of course—but the nightowl shearwater
Is mostly monogamous, and lives *en famille*
In nests that humans are not meant to see.
The shearwater is content with its own kind.
On nights when there's no moon, the Isle of Bardsey
Breaks its vow of silence, grows loud as a kennel,
As if nature itself were speaking its mind.

THE LAST NIGHT

The girls are mopping the painted stone floor.
Papá has set his boots by the door.

He gives instructions; they obey.
There were thirty seals in the harbor today.

The girls are playing at Pop Singer,
But I have hurt my ring finger

By falling into prickly gorse.
Papá so likes a clean house!

The baby goats are black-and-white.
Perhaps I shall not sleep tonight

For there's no moon this time of month
Despite the prayers of our mad monk,

And nesting choughs and shearwaters
Will cry, as I for my lost daughters.

LEARNING TO LIVE WITH STONE

A shore of washed stones
A sky the color of stone
A stone cliff

Stony face, stony heart

There is nothing here,
Twisted roots, sea taking the land
Back. Sea wrack
And rain.
                There is nothing
Here between us but stone.

One must learn to live with stone,
Make it a bed to lie on
A step to climb.

Carve.

The Life and Death of Poetry

The final section from *The Life and Death of Poetry*.

ON TRANSLATION

Be warned, I tell my students.
A writer with nothing to write
is in danger of falling into
one or more of four
pitfalls: drink, drugs,
adultery, and translation.

Drink will sink you. Drugs
don't even deserve discussion.
Adultery is too expensive
for the young and when you are old
it is too exhausting.
This leaves translation.

Now, then. I'm sure you know
that every translation
is an interpretation
and that interpretation
displays a point of view,
which you must have. Get one.

To translate, you will need
a dictionary of the language
from which you are translating
and a dictionary of the language
into which you will translate.
Also, something to translate,

hereinafter referred to
as the text. Begin with a text
that is relatively easy:
short, clear, shapely.
Of course, "short, clear,
shapely" won't guarantee

a relatively easy text.
Take Catullus, the "*Odi
et amo*": merely two lines
but impossible to unpack
in English. It's been done
but never well enough.

Once you have your text
you'll want to do a word-
by-word translation, taking
note of what can be carried
into, say, English, and what
must be abandoned by

the roadside: the meter? the rhyme?
the lavender thyme spilling
over the stone wall in
Auvillar? You must,
sometimes, prune the text
to make room for imagery

that branches out from the *vocab-
ulaire* of the language, French, say,
that you are translating.
Okay. You know already
that Frost said poetry is
what gets lost in translation,

and so it is, standing
there helplessly, its arms
by its sides as cars zoom by
and the sun lowers itself
into the blue bath of
evening. But it would be true,

too, to say that poetry
may be found in translation.
The flowering branches grow
into new, dynamic forms,
inscribing themselves on air,
their blossoms bright as flares.

A new poem has grown
next to the other, yet not
as volunteer (far-flung,
defiantly independent),
but as a companion of
the heart of the other, two—

and maybe many more—
entwined and reflecting one
another in the blue
pond of the evening sky.
And yes, perhaps there'll be
anachronisms here

or there, but, really, so what?
You are not writing the work
for the time for which the author
wrote it. In fact, you are not
writing the work at all.
You are not Catullus, not

Sophocles, although, translating
Antigone, you felt
such sympathy for her
and her stupid uncle
you truly thought you'd be
torn in half, both halves

thrown to wolves, as were they,
in a sense, given that
the narrative thread of the play
is closer to a noose.
I've always loved that play
but it's one of those loves that hurt.

Be warned, I tell my students.
To translate, you must love
the text, and if you love
the text, you will be led
down blind alleys, through dark
parks, to the jumping-off

place where your sore need,
your ravenous desire
bind you to the book
you left on the stone wall
bursting with lavender thyme—
small blossoms thickly scented.

Love finds us out, even
the love of words. To translate
is to penetrate the text
until it yields, unfolding
meaning and music and swoons
beneath your ballpoint pen.

My students smile. They think
I'm being salacious, or modishly
ironic, but I'm not.
I want to teach them that
a pitfall is a pitfall
is a black oubliette

they'll not get out of unless
they know what they are doing.
A text merits respect
and must be handled with care,
you must recognize its allurements
and dangers. A dangerous text?

Oh yes, if it keeps you from
the work you meant to be
your own. Remember this,
dear students, as you kiss
or smoke in the rising tide
of ever-deepening night:

Translation adds to who
you are but takes away
your self. The question is,
Will you give your life
for someone else's work?

God help you now.

WHAT THE POET WISHES TO SAY

What the poet wishes to say cannot be said,
in part because it has been said, and often,
before, but this was true when only the second
poet wrote. It becomes no truer with time.

The bigger reason the poet cannot say
what she wishes to say is that she wishes to say
something that seems to be a kind of music,
a word-field of music, as it's less a text
and more a space of time profoundly charged
by feeling, like the awe attendant to
our modest place among the huge events
of universal import: stars and novae,
the initiating burst of Many from
the One—the one what? Impacted point,
or god, or some computer-generated
simulacrum? In any case, the whole
of it.   If everyone could speak the whole,
then everyone would speak poetry, but
Molière's *gentilhomme* was perfectly pleased to learn
he had been speaking prose.
                              Even for those
whose language is poetry, the task requires
a life of: practice, contemplation, prayer.
(The latter two are sham without the first.)
This life begins in echo and extends
into apprenticeship, a period
that may be short or long but always ends,
if it ends, with the achievement of a vision
or "showing," as Julian of Norwich called her visions
of Jesus Christ, but we prefer "a view."
(Transported as we are by art and music,
the leap to faith remains a leap to faith.)
So say "a view," a world view if you must,
but know that you are only halfway home.
Even with the view. Even speaking poetry.
Because poetry is not the only language
you must master. You must also learn
the personal language that will convey your view,
and since your view, so similar to the ones

you love, also differs from them, if only
because the time in which you live and write
is different, you must invent that language,
hoping a few readers follow on the same
path and perhaps they will and perhaps they won't.
But how to make a language of your own?

In short, the process has to do with rhythm.
The racing rhymes of Dante's *terza rima*
so magnify the interlocking of
hell, earth, and heaven that the universe,
the medieval universe, becomes one verse.
And Chaucer's Wife of Bath is like a laugh
so full and deep it shakes the ground of England.
And Will, whose way with words created English,
creates as well the tense, or rueful, clash
between the life of action and the life
within the skull, that secret, teeming world.

Or consider a poet less removed
in time, whose reputation for that reason
is hard to know, yet Osip Mandelstam,
arrested and in exile, begging food
and blankets, honed the razor of his lines.
Discussing Osip, poet Joseph Brodsky
notes, "Whatever a work of art consists of,
it runs to the finale which makes for its form
and denies resurrection."
                         This is true
and not true, as it is, too, when he writes, "After
the last line of a poem, nothing follows
except literary criticism."
Both statements are rather more clever than correct.
What follows a poem is often a poem in response.
Or a poet may write a poem that enacts
its own resurrection.
                     As for the poet,
the poet aims not at immortality
of self or reputation but of what
he or she wishes to say, the world as it was,
or seemed to be, on that day in mid-October

when the hills were still green, the wildflowers
scattered like birdseed from a hand not seen
nor felt, and the various, changing, falling leaves
swirled up again, caught in a sudden updraft,
then settled on the ground like immigrants,
a huddling, a community of color.
A day when a small boy rushed to open the door
to shout "*Bonjour, Madame!*" to a woman whom
he'd never met and waked in her a feeling
of sheerest joy, salvific and abiding.
The poet wishes to say what life was like
here on the planet in the twenty-first
disturbing century and might, to do
so, think of her beloved Beethoven,
who, deaf and lonely, brought his art to such
sublimity, it is as if he wrote
his music among the spheres of music, working
at a desk of sky, the innumerable stars for lighting,
a gust of solar wind sending manuscript
flying. In the late piano sonatas,
you hear the composer placing his notes, solid
and silken as they somehow manage to be,
without hesitation but with deliberateness
exactly where they are supposed to go,
thereby fixing the apparatus of heaven
God had let fall idle.

THE LIFE AND DEATH OF POETRY

If word came into world
Taking the form of man,
Poetry is body,
Flesh and blood we read,
A text that, like a heart,
Can move a heart to love.

The poem's heart must be cradled
Live in a loving hand.
Through vein and artery
The blood of it will bleed
As though to make a desert
Bloom, like brightened grove.

If angels flocked to herald
The birth of the one God-man,
They surely sang sweetly, clearly.
Did wise men following the lead
Of a star discover the art
Of reading the word from above?

And were there years untold,
The boy left alone
To play and think and try
His elders, who agreed
He might grow into the part
Of a good man who could move

God to pity his people?
Grown, he would teach God's plan
Even to the Pharisee.
So the poem, as yet unread,
Allowed to mature apart
From hectoring world, will give

Itself time to be called
Into the world, a fan
Of palm waving wildly
Where sandy roads fed
Into the main artery.
In the sky, a white dove

Cried, unconsoled
By the crowd shouting hosannas
To the man riding a donkey.
Someone scattered seed
Onto a low rampart
But the bird did not dive

For it, would not be fooled
By cajolery or praise or paean;
Even a dove has a duty
To fulfill, can fill a need,
Bemoan the human heart.
At the last stop, it hove

Into the doorway, furled
Its wings, and perching on
A ledge, with its beauty
Welcomed the one who'd heed
Its presence, its trembling heart,
The one who saw it hover

Through supper then tuck its bold
Head, for the night's duration,
Beneath a wing, mutely
Dreaming of birds once treed—
Here the bird startled—
By flood let loose to save

Believers, but what ship's hold
Rescued the child or man,
The woman, guilty only
Of praying river would recede,
Of loving rock and root
And green moss grown over

The flood-enriched land, gold
Under returning sun?
Why must the innocent die?
No God, and no church creed,
Tells us, and yet his feet
Were lovingly laved

By Magdalene, her gold
Whore's heart opened
To receive his respectful pity.
Trusting, willing to accede
To his requirements, heart beating,
She bowed her head and prayed,

And what did he behold
In that deferential woman?
A citizen of his city,
The kingdom of God. Indeed,
As she washed his aching feet,
He saw she longed to be saved,

To be freed and paroled
From her history of sin,
As did everybody
He met who was not dead
To himself, who knew the part
That each of us has played

In others' lives, how we killed
Their hopes, how cruel we've been
Accidentally and may still be,
The words we've left unsaid
And those wielded artlessly,
A blunt and shredding blade.

Do we believe in a stone rolled
Back, in a resurrected man?
We believe in poetry.
We believe language is the blood
Of the Lamb and the heart
Of the Heart we must revive

Again and again. Christ, cold
And sleepless on the mountain,
May have been an epiphany—
Or a blasted tree hooded
In fog rising out
Of nightwood and leaving

Like a ghost or, dark and coiled,
Like the shameful smoke of the ovens,
Or both. The poem must die
To the poet, it must be dead
To the poet's ego, go out
Of the poet's self, cleaving

To time's cross, stretched and nailed,
Forgotten, to be reborn
In the human heart,
The poem as mustard seed,
The poem as a work of art
That will gloriously live.

Or not. Perhaps the world
Pays no serious attention.
It does not matter. Poetry
Is not the human reed
Broken into many parts
On the turning wheel of life.

While autumn leaves are whirled
By wind and schoolchildren
Drop from the branch of a tree
That overhangs a raked bed,
A patchwork quilt of sorts,
With the laughter of those who thrive

In homes tenderly ruled
By loving parents, sun
Low in the deepening sky,
The kids' hands chapped and red,
While our planet cartwheels
Toward winter, we are alive

To hear the parents scolding,
The children racing in,
Their shouts falling to reverie,
To see the last sun spread
Against the sky like fine art
And day turn to evening.

Poetry's just poetry. The world
Is where what is human
Matters more. The body
Is as helpless as a reed,
But it has a heart
A poem can move to love.

Gadgetry

"Gadgetry" is the second section in *Quartet for J. Robert Oppenheimer*. He is often described as the father of the atomic bomb. Represented in this section are his successes and difficulties with the development of the bomb, his friends, co-workers, and family, and the charge his country tasked him with: to make a bomb before Germany did.

THE VIRTUOUS DEAD

Near by the withered tree, a dried-up well
leads down to another world, in which the shades
of precursor Greeks and Romans carry on,
though listlessly, attenuated lives.
How do they come to be so far from home?

So deep beneath the battle-scarred surface of
the earth, there are no nationalities.
Men so old their tongues are thick with dust,
the heroes of the classical past, remember
better times, swap war stories and tales
of athletic feats on well-groomed playing fields.

Aeneas, with Anchises on his back,
observed the fall of Troy. A great city
dying strangles on its people's cries.

ON NOT WRITING A CATALOGUE OF SHIPS

A catalogue of ships seems called for, what
with all those battleships and aircraft carriers
and airships, and the fishing boats that got
refugees and spies safely to Sweden
or were instrumental to successful sabotage,
and including the names of generals, heroes,
and commanders, but unlike the ancient Greeks
we harbor our history in history books,
which is why there is no catalogue herein,
but do not forget that loose lips sink ships.

TWO NOT OF A KIND

General Leslie Groves knew he'd found
his man, equipped with enormous erudition,
a theoretical thinker dedicated
to verifiable truth, a persuasive talker
able to elicit the allegiance of
mechanics, engineers, and physicists
toward a single aim: the atomic bomb.

The scientists disliked the strong-arm general
but the general didn't give a shit. Scientists
were needed, Oppenheimer needed, himself
the General needed, and that was all that mattered,
though promotion to Brigadier General
helped him to reach that contented conclusion.

As for Oppenheimer, he saw in Groves a guy
who'd support his scientific director and
whose tolerance for red tape barely exceeded
his own.
        The one a bulky ship against
the sky, the other a vanishingly thin contrail.

OPPENHEIMER AND THE DEAN OF ST. PAUL'S CATHEDRAL

Batter my heart, three person'd God. . . .
   —John Donne

Tatlock introduced him to the poems of Donne,
that man of steely mind and passionate heart.
It was a meeting of like souls. He shared
Donne's penchant for yoking opposites
together, for seeing the sides of every problem,
for polarities that bend like Moebius strips,
and paradox that causes us to open
wider our always narrowly focused eyes.
As Oppenheimer loved the poems of Donne,
so Donne loved science, and as Donne loved science,
so Oppenheimer loved the poems of Donne.

NEW MEXICO

The sky was wide open, a type of range
where roamed not antelope but a sun as orange
as pumpkins and white cloudlets like wild ponies.
Strings of sizzling red peppers against adobe
exterior walls reminded him of *mezuzahs*,
with their parchment prayers, nailed to doorposts in cases
often striking in their close-worked elegance,
though he was not observant, nor given to
religiosity beyond the usual
feelings of awe and oneness that attended
the scientific facts of his profession.
He liked the heady, horizontal space
of this place, which balanced the soaring ambition of
the reason he was here. The Sangre de Christo
mountains lifted and relieved his inward gaze,
resettled it upon the distant peaks.
The snap in the air caused his blue eyes to widen;
in them, a reflection of the galloping sky.

SOME SAY

That Hitler was compensating for having only one testicle.
That Hitler contracted syphilis from a Jew
and this was why he turned against the Jews.
That when his half-niece died he was broken-hearted
and crossed over into madness. That his madness
was genetically determined. That he compensated
for his failure as an artist by creating
an artistic design for genocide. Let us

say: hatred and envy riddled his heart and mind
like a disease, leaving vacant the places where
good sense and kindness might otherwise have lodged.

NEWSREEL

His wife was known to take a drink or two
or five or six with women friends as day
drove on toward pointless evening.
It's plausible that Oppie scorned their chatter.
Besides which, the day was deathly hot. Why not,
he thought, escape into an air-conditioned
movie theater?

                In black-and-white,
the news precedes the film. He is face to face
with Jews behind barbed wire. It makes him sick.
He flees up the aisle to the men's room. Washes his face,
his hands, then dries them with a paper towel.
He wants nothing more than to drop the bomb
on Germany. He wants to blow Germany
off the fucking planet. He does not feel
less sick but at least no one can decipher
what has hit him. That is how he prefers
to be seen, or rather, not be seen. He is
a man of feeling afraid of feeling.

ON NOT WRITING THE HOLOCAUST

No poet who was not there can describe
the horror of the camps. We may recite
what we have read, or learned from videos,
but no one will be satisfied with a poem
by one who was not there. The poet may
describe the hellholes where people starved daylong
in darkness and isolation, the way they were treated
as worse than plague-ridden rats, the suffocating
smell of decayed or burnt flesh, but no one
will accept the poem as adequate. Therefore,
the poet concedes to historians and those
who were there—Primo Levi, Elie Wiesel—
the art of description, yet even so the poet bears
those images in her mind and they weigh
on her like ash and bone and cold, cold earth
thrown upon mass graves of the dead and still alive.

JEWS

The burnt. The starved. The buried alive.
Electrocution-by-fence. Experiments.
The snapped neck, the spinebroke back. The hanged.
Death by gas. Disease.
So many ways of killing the Jews.
Poison. Bayonet. Work
that made no one free. We can only bow our heads,
we who were not there. Should you meet
a Jew coming through the rye, shake his hand
for he has traveled far and into life
with stalwart heart and knowledge of the worst
humanity can do. Humanity?
Shouldn't we find another word for what
we are? This poem is open to suggestions.

LOS ALAMOS

The bridge by which the outer world could breach
the hidden city still is in place, a narrow
wooden-plank affair, as tenuous
as a hypothesis and yet triumphant,
though a newer bridge parallels the old.
For the site of Los Alamos, Oppenheimer
had chosen Pajarito Plateau, miles high
above sea level, volcanic mesa on which
a school was converted into the scientists' base camp.

The Project personnel now took it over.
They came on buses painted olive-drab,
the army's favorite color. The constant noise
of building drummed, heightening expectations,
like the soundtrack to a movie. Something big
was going on, and they would be a part
of it. The mystery and the magic of
their being there transformed them into soldiers,
allied with one another and alive
to the sun, the earth, the rocks and trees and air.

THE GADGET

His former student Robert Serber, now
a colleague, tasked with bringing up to speed
the scientists arriving in Los Alamos
almost daily, lisped perceptibly.
Even so, the lectures—on nuclear fission
 —were a triumph, a brilliantly abbreviated
summation of what they knew at that point,
as clear and cogent as a syllogism.
The blackboard was on wheels and chalkdust flew
like snow, sawdust pouring from the ceiling.
Serber looked up. He saw a foot. The foot
had broken through the floor above. He went on
with his talk, but the outsider's foot, now inside the room,
reminded Oppenheimer of the need
for security. We know this, as he quickly
dispatched a different colleague to the front of the room
with a message to Serber, who, midspeech, began
referring to the "gadget," though he'd been calling it
the "bomb." What if the man with the foot through
the ceiling had been a spy? the scientists asked,
chuckling among themselves.

                              Twenty-five
years later, after Oppenheimer died,
Serber, now a widower, set out
with Kitty O. to sail around the world
in her fifty-two-foot ketch *The Moonraker*
that skimmed the silver light of Caribbean seas
but Kitty died at Panama Canal.
The man had loved all three: his wife, his boss,
his boss's wife. And science too, of course.
A scientist's love for science is intimate
and true.

THE NIGHT HE SPENT WITH TATLOCK AT HER APARTMENT IN SAN FRANCISCO

Depressed, and bisexual in America
when women in America could not own
openly their bisexuality,
Jean Tatlock called on Oppenheimer to
protect her from herself. He stayed the night.
J. Edgar Hoover thought *disloyalty*
and *lust*, *betrayal* and *unworthiness*,
though many men have stayed a night to talk
a woman out of death by pills or poison,
revolver, hanging, gas, or suffocation.
Despairing women ask that men embrace
them chastely, and sensitive men will do just that.
But Hoover, though a creep, had got it right,
and six months later Tatlock drowned herself.
Her father found her cold wet corpse.
                                              Half
a year can hold a holiday, some books,
some favorable weather, birdsong, a child on a tricycle,
a good idea, and the joy of music. One hopes.

NIGHT

Full moon. And in a quadrant of the sky
Orion hunts, his dogs at heel. Venus,
lonely, shimmers in her satin nightgown.
Bodies like these make human bodies small,
eccentric things, playthings perhaps, like dolls
and Yo-yos. The human body is soft, unshelled.
Planetary bodies obey laws of
physics. After dark, in lighted rooms,
the scientists pushed one another to work
harder, harder. Piñion and juniper
sharpened the night air to a brilliant point.
The brilliant scientists sketched their brilliant thoughts
in quick equations on the blackboard, and
Oppenheimer approved, or squashed mistakes.
Outside, beneath the moon, an armadillo,
soft beneath its leathery armor, crossed streets
and gentle-hearted drivers braked.

DESPONDENCY

A friend found him slumped, with head in hands,
at his desk, clearly bone-tired and deeply despondent,
the substance of him frayed and verily shredded.
So still was he, he might have been a sculpture
by Giacometti called *Man Slumped at Desk*.
Light from the window slept on the desktop, like
a cat. Dust motes swam in the stream of light,
the bookmark in a book silent as a stone,
dropped paperclip dusty and unnoticed on the floor.
Imagine the look of consternation on
the face of his friend. Imagine the swarm of thoughts
in Robert's heavy head. Was it Tatlock,
his swooning, complicated Dido, who
despaired of justice, beauty, any hope
the world would heal from war's gravest wounds?
Was it the FBI, which spied on them,
voyeurs and tattletales, automatons
who have no understanding of emotion?
Was it the sick-making pressure of his job?
Or was it home life, private matters sealed
off from onlookers, those daily encounters and
confrontations that occur when no one's looking,
that spies don't realize are consequential
(although the phones at home and work were tapped)?
It seemed he'd never lift his head or rise,
a phoenix, from that sunbathed desk again.

THE TEAHOUSE AT OTOWI STATION

The chocolate cake was famously fabulous
but Edith, worried Tilano might imbibe,
banned liquor from her dinner table. "Los
Alamosers," as she called them, carpooled,
boozing before and after. A piñon fire,
fresh corn, a chicken wrung by the neck by her
or by Tilano, peas and squash and beans—
and raspberries on the chocolate cake, the cake
served with strong black coffee in pottery mugs.
On another day she wrote, *I saw a cloud*
pass over the earth on long grey stilts of rain.

DIDO RELEASED TO THE WINDS

At last omnipotent Juno, out of pity
For Dido's artless, shameless lovesickness,
Her physical pain, and her desire to join
Her husband in the afterworld, commissioned
Iris to deliver Dido from such suffering
Unto death, which was not possible
Until Proserpine received a lock
Of Dido's lovely hair. Then Iris flew
Down from Olympus on saffron wings bedewed
And refracting the thousand colors that compose
Sunlight and with her right hand cut the lock
From Dido's hair. "As I have been commissioned,
I give this lock to Dis, releasing you
From your body's agony." Therewith the warmth
Of that body fled into the wide world's winds
And Dido was cold, cold to the touch, and untouched.

[*The Aeneid* IV, 11. 693—705]

DIDO IN THE FIELDS OF LAMENTATION

The Fields of Lamentation are the home
In death of persons love has misused and
Abused. Here they hide in glades of myrtle,
Grief clinging to them like their own shadows,
They wander, lost forever. Aeneas looks,
And there, among the others, is his Dido,
The Phoenician, her sword-wound fresh as a new rose.
Or so he thinks, in the twilight haze in which
Deer bound silently and mostly unseen.
Tears drenched his face as he spoke to her:
                                        "Dido,

Dido, then the message is true and you are dead,
A suicide. Was it because of me?
Dear Queen, I swear I never would have left
You, never you, had not the gods willed it.
And it's because of them that I am here
Now, a visitor to this darkling realm
Where no bird sings and no one laughs. Dido,
I never meant to cause you such awful suffering.
Wait! Don't go! Are you afraid of me?
This is our last chance to speak together!"

And so he sought to calm her agitated
Shade, but Dido would not return his look,
Only stared at the ground. She was like a statue,
And then she was gone, having fled back to
The glades and groves, and the arms of her late husband,
Sychaeus. Had she heard a word of what
He said? She'd been so cold to him. And more:
Her fate seemed so unfair, and in his heart
He pitied her.

[*The Aeneid* VI, 11. 440-476]

NIGHTS IN THE SECRET CITY

Average age: 29. Bathtubs:
five. Lab alcohol: two-hundred proof
and though it mixes with water molecules
as soon as you open the bottle, it packs a punch.
Dorm dances, dinner parties, small flirtations
or wild improbable sexual liaisons.
The body wants what the body wants, and minds
alive with learning want what the body wants,
mind and body being a natural twosome.
A lot of fun was had. Feynman slapped
the bongo drums to exorcise the grief
he felt for his late beloved wife. Mountains
crammed with *los alamos*— "the cottonwoods"—
officiated like benign sentinels
undisturbed by human behavior. The sky, that sky
that stretches over the southwestern world,
like a god with a million eyes who lies awake
at night, may well have been somewhat amused.
The earth is small, its people smaller, and
tragedy perhaps merely a minor scene
in a much longer comedy.

THE OFFICE WIFE

A woman might drown herself in those blue eyes,
might rive her heart on his razor-sharp cheekbones
or immolate herself in his fevered mind.
Do I exaggerate? Ask Dorothy
McKibben, keeper of the gate—the entrance
to the secret city—and Oppenheimer's helpmate
in almost everything, even taking
his wife off his hands, or to Albuquerque.
It takes a woman to do that—devote
her life to a man who'd never belong to her.
But think of her importance to the project,
think how the days flew by like snowflakes caught
in a great flailing upward gust of wind.

OMAHA BEACH

The generals had done their math,
calculating X number of bodies
equal to one man alive for long
enough to get somewhere, for howsoever
short a time. And how long did it take
for troops to know that those first off the boats
were getting "slaughtered like hogs," someone said,
which meant stunned, eviscerated, cut, and deboned
or possibly just shot all to hell.
Some must have counted themselves fortunate
to survive with no arms or no legs or
only blinded by blood geysering from
the stomach wound only one guy over
or burned but only on one side of
his strip-mined, and exploded, cratered face.

The boys who did the fighting had to fight
not only Germans but their own unsayable fears,
their understanding that they were about
to die. Victory? It was victory
over more than the taking of a beach.
It was a terrible victory over the self.

SONNET FOR A B-17

The B-17 takes a hit in its third engine,
the propeller of which begins irrationally windmilling.
No nearby airstrip, and "too goddamn dark
to see the stars," the pilot says. He manages

to stay aloft for a couple of hundred miles,
losing altitude all the while, of course.
He reaches the Warsaw city park and crash
lands, taking out trees and shrubs. On all sides

young Polish soldiers materialize, rifles
aimed and cocked. Not one of the kids speaks English.
Just then, a Russian officer rides up
in a jeep and tells the boys to put down their rifles.

No one is hurt.
This is the kind of war story we like.

FDR / R.I.P.

Franklin Delano Roosevelt was dead.
All that night, snow fell in the Secret City.
The roofs of Bathtub Row—shrouded in white.

The town thought the world a carpet pulled
out from under them, the way a blizzard
whites out the horizon, vertigo taking hold.

Oppenheimer too had felt that spinning,
spinning out of control. His mouth was dry,
his hands on the shaky side of nervousness

as he stepped on stage. Offering consolation
to the inconsolable was not his strength.
They sat in rows in the movie theater,

waiting while he stood at the front and worried.
Well, he took a breath—a very deep breath—
and straightened his skinny-ass self to his six feet plus.

AN IDLE MOMENT SOME DAYS BEFORE THE TRINITY TEST

The low steady hum of fluorescent light,
the office deserted now except for one man
who wanders over to the open window,
listens to the locusts' soft shrilling
and looks up at the stars, which get top billing
in the desert night.

WHITE SANDS

A turquoise sky, its overflowing light
splashing down on buttes, mesas, mountains,
ravines, arroyos, canyons, caves, and flats,
white sands where scaffolding abuts the sun
and engineers are measuring the space
between annihilation and the view.
Oppie's porkpie hat shadows his face.
(A skinny rabbit wisely leaps out of his way.)
He's nervous, tense, afraid that something will
go wrong—there is so much that even now
can go wrong. There is the question of fallout.
He hugs himself while smoking, arms crossed,
a pose so characteristic, so often noted,
that actors who play him do the same. The flood
of light is only a metaphor, of course.
In general, deserts are dry, and men
measuring white sands are a mirage.

DESERT FLOWERS

All those men roaming the southwest desert—
soldiers with machine guns plugging antelope,
engineers building bunkers and a crate,
scientists in a state approaching hysteria,
and all of them, all of them, taking leaks.
It is a wonder the desert didn't stink,
that ocotillo and yucca managed to survive.
(The urine must have dried immediately.)
When Oppenheimer strolled off for a discreet piss,
he strolled back with a debonair air and a desert flower
in hand to offer to whoever was there.

THE STORM

The towering shot tower treacherous with run-off
from the storm, cable banging in the wind,
ice picks of lightning slashing the bold-faced sky
and one poor guy to guard the site against
sabotage though no saboteurs turned up
that night, thank heavens. Thank too the thoroughly soaked
single guard. Around the tower's base:
mattresses, in case the gadget fell,
or a scientist. The cable kept on clanging,
Oppenheimer couldn't sleep. General
Groves slept like a well-fed, overlarge baby.
I. I. Rabi showed up in a black homburg,
umbrella in hand, and when the storm moved off
the sky grew clear as the clearest of complexions,
suffused with dawning pink.

EMILY DICKINSON AT TRINITY

the flash
the mushroom cloud
the loud devouring roar

zero at the bone
fire at the core

TRINITY

A thunderstorm wracked their scaffolding on the night
before the test. It might have been bad luck,
it might have been the anger of the gods,
but then the weather cleared as dawn approached,
crawling from the cave of unremembered time
like a child attempting first steps.
                              Trinity
was the name Oppenheimer gave to the site,
perhaps in tribute to Tatlock or Donne or
the *Bhagavad Gita*. Or all of those.
The time was five thirty a.m. Only
Oppenheimer wore a coat; it was
July. He also wore a suit, the suit
now baggy, the man's body emaciated.
He also wore his porkpie hat. He leaned
into a post. Wiped his face. "Lord,"
he said, "these affairs are hard on the heart."
His old *bête noir*, anxiety, clouded
his face until "it was lit by reflections from
the sand," says Abraham Pais, of what
some saw as Oppenheimer's triumphant glow
that monumental day.

TONGUES OF FLAME

Cross the river
Go down through fire
The hero's mother burns
on the eternal pyre

Odysseus was in hell,
seeing his mother's shade

brighter than a thousand suns
they said, after the blast
after the conquering future
became the uncorrectable past,

Who shall be saved?
Already, the tongues of flame
lick the backs of his hands,
saying his name

TRINITITE

Nearsighted, you might at first think grass has grown
at Trinity Site, the desert a lawn, the lawn
a lunch for Nebuchadnezzar. These bits of green
are trinitite, sand alchemized to glass
by bomb blast. Or *say a sea-change rich
and strange*. What Oppenheimer knew before
the bomb was not what he knew afterward—
truth too easily forgot. *Between
the idea and the reality falls
the shadow* of a doubt, as Eliot
might have written—should have written, if
he'd been honest with himself. The present poet
shores these fragments against her crumbling heart.
We can't put back what physics rips apart.

TWO PRELUDES AND A BOMB

On Sugar Loaf Hill on Okinawa
the mud in which American soldiers slipped
and fell face first was rich with maggots and feces.
Twelve thousand Marines died in that fucked-up muck.

A Japanese submarine torpedoed
the USS *Indianapolis*, which sank
in twelve minutes. Four days and five nights,
with no food, no water, American sailors struggled
to escape the sharks that picked them off and dragged
them down through black water. Out of their minds,
they were, imagining the Officers' Quarters—
and drinkable water—lay on the bottom of
the ocean.

      August 6, the *Enola Gay*
delivered Little Boy to Hiroshima.
If any kind of God existed, surely
he would have been ashamed to show his face,
which means there was no God around that day
though there were people trying to help people
and maybe people like that are a kind of God
or church. Tsutomu Yamaguchi, a man
of business, burned by the bomb in Hiroshima,
traveled home to Nagasaki just in time
to be irradiated by the bomb
code named Fat Man.

AUGUST 5, 1945

The boy perched on the steps.
The day was as clear as the child's eyes,
a day made for perching on steps.

After the bomb, the boy is gone—
not fishing, not to school, not
called by family or playmate,

just gone, his shadow burnt
into those stone steps,
himself mere air.

At the same moment,
language comes to an end.

We cannot speak, our voices crack
and break, our tongues stumble
through the ruins of the tower of Babel.

PIKADON (FLASH BOMB)

The blast boiled flesh from bone,
ground bone to grit, flake, and shard.

What more is there to say?

White light in silence,
the moment suspended—
a woman changed to air—

What more is there to say?

Like a dog with a bone
winds shook the city.

What more is there to say?

A man carried his eyes in his cupped hands,
palms open, as though his hands might see
what he could not.

The still living
envied the dead.

What more is there to say?

Black rain fell.
What more?

The sickness began.

AFTERWARD

He said to Truman, "Mr. President,
I feel I have blood on my hands." From that,
we know that first he asked himself, *Did I
cause this?* Was he a murderer? A killer
of children? "We have known sin," he also said.
If anyone has sinned, retorted Bridgeman,
it's God, by making fission possible.
Meanwhile, Truman was having none of it.
The blood, said Truman, was on his *presidential*
hands, and he was not the sniveling showoff
Oppie was. What Oppenheimer could not
say was that he meant *My poor daughter*,
and *poor daughter* stood for all the children
in this fallen world that he had changed and that
he could not change back.

THE NATURE OF WAR

Of course he had blood on his hands. Who did not?
Everyone did, including pacifists,
who let others do the killing. It is the nature
of war to spill like a river over banks
into the ground on which we walk, infecting
every one of us with sin. Is *sin*
too theological a word? Say *crime*,
as in *crimes against humanity*. A war
anywhere seeps into our hearts, our veins
flushed with worrisome discomfiture and remorse.
A good war, we say, and we are profoundly grateful
to those who won it. And yet—

PITY OUR MYTHS

> *Pity our myths. . . .*
> —Oppenheimer, as quoted by David Lilienthal

Pity our myths, for they are few and frail
and tear like Christmas paper, sputter out
like Sabbath candles. What we think we know,
we know not. The blue-eyed Buddha escaped
earth's sorrow by achieving enlightenment
but where does that leave us? Sending troops
overseas—Pacific, Atlantic, Caspian—
wherever blood is spilled, wherever it flows
in the firmament. The beautiful classical gods
age badly, splendid talents gone to seed,
their once-fabulous lives reduced to routine.
And the myths of the North, of a race of mighty men
and strong women with gold-spun hair and rings
that gleam in musky moonlight, who tells them now,
and who would want to, knowing where they lead?
Poor myths indeed, worn to bare bone, clacking
the same old same old, while yet the scientists
are telling us of new discoveries,
the strangest tales of all, narratives of
materials, measurement, gravity, and mind.

WAR

Like Aeneas, like Achilles,
quite like the warrior-kings of old,
a leader calls together strategists
and makers of arms and bearers of arms.
Thus did Oppenheimer, not in revenge
or excess but to save civilization
from the brute mindlessness of Fascism.
Can anyone think that Oppenheimer was *not*
shocked by what he'd done? That he was un-
perturbed by all the dead, the obliterated, the burned,
the maimed, the scarred, the sick, the suffering,
the irradiated, the deformed, the mourning
of Hiroshima and Nagasaki? He was human.
His wife clasped his hand.
She stroked his head.
She waited for his coughing fit to stop
and steadied him. A melting blaze slid down
the west to rise in the land of the rising sun.
We know that war perpetuates itself,
that cruelty has lasting consequences,
but we don't know anything that he didn't know.
Life finds us between a rock and if not
a very hard place then an empty place,
abyss, black hole, the void, or Avernus
where Persephone withdrew to winter with Hades.
We learn to live without assurances.

Beholder's Eye

Beholder's Eye collects poems about places where I lived or visited, or in other words, it is about where I went and what I saw. Culling from these poems, I shall stick with the places that most amazed or enchanted or disturbed or interested me.

AESTHETICS

Composition and perspective
Can make of almost anything
A work of art, except perhaps
The highway accident—charred

Chassis dismembered by the jaws
Of life, ambulance screaming
As if in pain. Horror is not
Beautiful nor sublime, nor does

It illumine or expand the world,
Yet artists have painted beautiful paintings
Of human decay and degradation
And as for jaws of death, some find

Beauty in a circling shark.
Can ugliness be beautiful?—
But this is not a new question,
And there are those who answered *yes*,

Like Francis Bacon and Damien Hirst.
I cannot say that I agree,
Although Bacon's figuration
Of ageing makes us grieve for our lack

Of compassion, and that is salutary,
I suppose. Yes, definitely
Salutary. But beauty, I think,
Is built on ambiguity,

Nuance, contour and tessitura,
Layers of meaning and levels of
Understanding, also on
The opposite of what is said,

Made, sung, built, arranged,
Choreographed, connections threaded
Through the whole to unify
The parts of what it adds up to.

Beauty is in search of wholeness,
A sense of life that brings together
The myriad tools of creation
In a single creation. Beauty reveals

Itself in actual completion.
It is not process. It is concretion.

ART BY MATISSE

Matisse makes paintings dance and colors run.
A picture on a wall will bend and stretch
And touch its toes if it is by Matisse.
Matisse's dancers spin, or they are spun
By the master's sleight of hand and exquisite eye
That balance the world on the tip of a loaded brush.
Color is everywhere except in air
Left unpainted or cut out of cut-out
Representations, and oh! the goldfish in
The fishbowl, how it shines like a lesser star,
How it glides behind glass, a golden glissade.

BIRKENAU

An expanse of green that could be called a meadow.
Willows and birches with noiseless birds on their branches.

A tenuous hush like a hive of bees sleeping.
Or icebergs before they encounter the *Titanic*.

A massive silence. Beneath the susurrus
Of breeze, the murdered murmur, their reaching voices
Below the surface of the ground and just
Below the registry of sound. Unheard,
Then, but we feel their immolated weight—
And keen and caustic edges—like bricks and stones
Thrown at the living, who, no matter how
They try, can never be sufficiently
Ashamed of what they did or didn't do.
We who walk here in remembrance know
That even though the dead feel nothing, not
Cold and neither warmth, what the millions dead
Must most bitterly miss is sensation.
Visitors pressing an ear to railroad tracks
Might pick up echoes of earth's wounded heart,
The heavy haul of it, a loaded truck,
Its beat irregular, arrhythmic. At
The memorial: flowers, lighted candles.
On the outer side of each trestle of train track:
A red rose.

BLUE RIVER

The Daugava, on which Riga is sited,
Flows serenely through the singing city.
Thus that sweet but complicated city
Is, by that ancient river, bluely lighted.
The opera house, so grand, so prideful and
Beloved, presents symphonic masterpieces
Or otherwise entertains. In bits and pieces
The history of an often conquered land
Comes clear, or clearer: the Baltic barons; kings
Of Sweden; Soviet Russia's heavy hand.
They had to shake it off, that grasping hand.
A country with a cultural tradition of singing
Breaks free, the city to be itself, the river
To sail cross country on its one blue wing.

IN RUSSIA

Canals in St. Petersburg
Reflect Italianate architecture,
Eighteenth-century windows wavering
Palely beneath water.

The first time I was there
This glimmering beauty seized me
By the throat, teased me
Like a promise, perhaps

A promise of adventure,
St. Isaac's Cathedral fabulous
As fairy tales, the Hermitage
A palace of paintings.

The second time I saw
Peter's playful gardens, fantastic
And intricate, with tiny, spastic
Fountains and flowers.

The third time I went
As part of an exchange,
Clouds burlier,
Weather changing.

Sidetrip to Yasnaya Polyana

> The walk to Tolstoy's grave
> Was beautiful and grave,
> Allée of broad-leaved lime,
> Trees a covered nave.

Three times—and now they seem
A single dream
As if I rowed a simple boat
Gently down a stream.

CROSSING THE FIELD

Madness of wind, catalpas lightning-lit
Like silverpoint, guttural rage of thunder,
The world in turmoil, wet and threatening.
Cattle huddle; depressions flood; clothes
Not taken in in time flap on the line,
Dancing a *danse macabre*. The distance from
Here to there is immense and seems
Unbreachable. The first required footstep
Takes years of training. The one that follows leads
To destinations unknown: San Antonio
Or New Jersey or an apartment on
The West Side. The third takes even longer
Than the first, and the fourth brings us to the gate,
Rusted, locked, and ivied, where we wait.

DRAGONFLY

I was five or six or seven, maybe eight.
Ithaca was a tough, cruel town
Back then. Disheartened students sometimes leapt
Off the bridge, which thus was known as Suicide Bridge,
But the day our parents took us for a picnic
Cascadilla Gorge was warm, the river
Clean and shining like a well-scrubbed aluminum pot.
Upstream, beside the Cornell tennis courts,
The water spread out like a tablecloth,
Relaxed and almost idle, though by the time
It reached the bridge, it was tricksy, tumbling,
Acrobatic, and still farther downstream
It slowed around wide flat rocks and cattails
Between low banks, and that was where we were,
My mother bra-less in a white tee-shirt
And pleated shorts, her legs shapely and long,
My handsome father sporting a moustache.
My father was afraid of me, as in
His generation many fathers were—
Confused about their daughters' femininity,
The delicious hair, the impossibly small wrists,
Their mystifying moods, their utter dependence,
The altogether strangeness of the genre.
I seldom saw my father; he supported
His family by working days and nights
And weekends; violinists were not a priority
In a country trying to recover from
The Great Depression and the Second World War.
But now here he was, crouching beside
Me, which made me the taller of us two.
"A dragonfly," he said, pointing at
A whirling dervish, a thing made mostly of air,
A body like a short straw, and stilt legs
Angled like a cable-stayed bridge and not much good
For walking on, the transparent wings
Unstoppingly busy as a hummingbird.
It hovered like a helicopter, inches
From my face, from his face too: a tiny dragon
Shimmering like a darning needle in sun,
A thing like music, motivated by
Love and the laws of biophysics.

ECLIPSE

A ring of fire remains but that is all.
All else is as it must have been before
The first—the very first, and shocking—dawn.
No shadow, only unrelieved nullity.
If you had eyes, they would not be of use.
If you could see, you still could not see.
Then light blossomed in the sky, flowered
Into dawn, and color, shape, and shadow
Announced their presence, to our endless joy.
Yet not endless: eclipses show us that
The dark has not been banished but persists
And will return when it chooses to return.

FRIENDSHIP

The elephant who loved the dog who loved
The elephant has brought the body of
The dog back home, wrapped in her loving trunk.
The two were friends for years, inseparable.
Dog let Elephant rub her belly with
Her huge, careful foot, unafraid.
Elephant and Dog spent hours side by side
In the sanctuary watching birds and rabbits.
Or Elephant watched Dog chasing birds and rabbits,
Unsuccessfully, of course. Languid clouds
Drifted with a lulling indifference.
Occasional breezes whispered in their ears.

Love between species is as true a love
As that of light for the dark, which is perseverant
And ever hopeful even though the light
Can never know the dark nor the dark light.

FULL MOON

Lavender sky, enormous pumpkin moon
Leaning low over hackberry, pine, and bamboo
On Old Mountain Road, Danville to Halifax,
Virginia. Deer slip in and out of dusk.
Surely the moon has left its orbit behind
And is about to smash into green earth,
Chasing the seas from their confining beds,
Worldwide tsunamis, people praying in panic,
Presidents and prime ministers herded
By underlings into underground shelters.
But no: before we have arrived back home
The moon has scaled the sky and shrunk, a small
Yellow disk now, but still perfectly round,
Still shadowing the deer on the ground.

GEOGRAPHY

The three principal products of Peru—
Does anyone remember them who's not
Enrolled in elementary school? *Textiles*
Is usually a good guess, and *oil*
Should American troops be deployed in
The particular exotic country under
Discussion.
              Cities of great importance tend
To be located on rivers and gulfs, where goods are traded,
But mountain ranges, soothing to behold,
Interfere with communication, and
May be the source of stressful isolation.
Topography is various and never
Less than interesting and yet the same
Can be said of staying in a single place
For a lifetime,
              In which case changes will be temporal,
Your family and friends growing older,
Weaker, sicker, sadder, broker, dumber,
Although those days you sit on your front porch
You don't regret not being in Peru.

HELSINKI

It snowed in summer in Helsinki,
Nights white, the unsetting sun a hail-
Mary to mania. I was
Interviewing survivors of
The Siege of Leningrad in
Their anonymous apartments. Not
A blizzard, not even a snowstorm,
Just small bright flakes from a sky
Clearing to blue. I recorded
The interviews on microcassettes.
Sometimes I recorded my notes, too.
This was before everyone
Walked and texted all day long.
Pre iPods, for that particular matter.
People looked at me as if
I were crazy, and maybe I was—
Tears on my face; talking to
Myself—but Helsinki is
A beautiful city, made for walking.
Survivors' stories of soaking wood
Glue bricks to mix with pearl barley
Or slurping saltbush-and-nettle soup
Were immensely sad and unsettling.
Those who agreed to be interviewed
Lived in a kind of recessive lighting
And spoke in low, soft tones as if
Reluctant to be heard. When
The snow stopped, day was bright as night.

INDIGO BUNTING

A shy fellow, despite his stunning plumage
Of Caribbean blue, and might his song
Be lightly inflected by a Jamaican accent?
A tinct of reggae?

                        He favors the liminal
But can be coaxed to partake of dinner at the feeder
Although a moving shadow will scare him off.
Therefore, do not move while he is dining.

That blue—as if he carries the Atlantic Ocean
On his back. As if coffee plantations call
To him. As if the sky through which he sails
Reflects the calm or rampant sea, a mirror
Image, a blue as deep as history.

THE JEWISH CEMETERY IN PRAGUE

The tombstones tumble over one another,
So close and many are they, earth engaged
With earth, a wrestling match among the dead.

The Jewish Quarter smells of warm rye bread.
Elsewhere in Prague, the young are hip and gay
But we admire the slower pace of those

Who don't imagine they are in a race
With what is trending, and we cross a street
That curves and drops downhill and brings us to

A favorite café, where no one cares
How long we linger in its cabbage warmth,
Its Czech chatter, the loud continuing clatter

Of plates and bowls and spoons. How good is life
That nourishes itself, persevering.

KRAKOW

The wind across the Square
Stopped only to tangle a tourist's hair

And convince another to buy a pair of gloves.
The day was cold with flashes of light on window panes
And pigeons and doves in search of handouts.

The clock tower watched, as clock towers will,
And the clock ticked three.

Here Oskar Schindler sheltered imperiled Jews
At his enamelware plant. Here the Vistula
Kisses the ankles of the Carpathian Mountains.

Here, as elsewhere, the weather is always new
Whereas history gets older and older.

LIGHT ON A WINDOWSILL

Light on the bright white windowsill
A sky blued and as fresh-smelling as jonquils
Washed in rain   Such happiness
As this must be illegal   I'll
Stroke your forehead, remove the helmet
And heavy, bronze greaves   I'll strip you
Of your battle-torn tunic   Gods will
Wonder why you and not they receive
My tenderest attentions   They will watch
 With envy in their hearts

MERIDA

Too Anglo to sit still for a siesta
I roamed the streets of Merida, city
Of sun and open markets and museums,
The stone buildings with Spanish arches grand
Yet discreet, a model of good manners.
In early evening everyone assembled
In the posada, on benches beneath old trees
With spreading, leafy branches, the first of the stars
Strung like piñatas from the velveteen sky.
The city seemed to wear a signature fragrance,
Something light and elegant, purchased in Paris,
Imported here, where a woman could disappear
For a week or two or three, shucking off
Controlling men, or a controlling man,
And dine alone *al fresco* on red snapper
Caught that afternoon and have a glass
Of wine in which the moon lingered like
A bantam beach ball or Lilliputian anchor.

(Yucatán)

METEOROLOGY

Today the sky looked like a sketch of the sky,
Like a sheet of white paper with charcoal clouds.
It would be fine to think that God drew it.
He didn't. We have meteorology
To thank. And when a blue sky sails over
Us, blue schooner tacking on blue sea, or
When the sky is smeared with rain or blizzards white
Out the horizon so there is no up
Or down, that too is meteorology.
But when the sky catches fire from a flash
So blinding that it turns your eyes to ashes
Or rains acid rain or traffics in toxins
That strangle to death every living thing
We'll have ourselves, and only ourselves, to thank,
Or rather, won't.

THE MINOTAUR NOW

A bull-muscled sea gores a pebbled shore
Wave upon wave, wearing away limestone,
Shale, glittering granite, and dolomite.
Scrub pine pesters the hillside and sunlight
Exposes the sea's sinewy currents. Creatures
Of the island sigh or murmur or mutter words
Unknown and silence smothers every sound.

The monster in his labyrinth, slain
By Theseus, sent his spirit into the sea,
Where Poseidon gave him freedom to roam as he wished
Where no man sees, or thinks him monstrous. He moves
The waters, carries them on his road-broad back,
Makes them rise and fall. His sharp hoofs paw
The ocean bed. His shoulders thrust against the shore.

NEW MEXICO INSTITUTE OF MINING AND TECHNOLOGY

The wind drove through the town like cars with fins
And atmospheric physicists rallied
On roof tops to measure velocity
And barometric pressure. Like gods they seized
The fractured bolts of lightning with their fists.
This was in the Eisenhower fifties
When women and girls were girls but boys were men.
There was one canteen in that desert town.
No dress shop. No Cineplex. No music
Unless somebody owned a record collection.
I listened to Franck and read Pasternak.
My Jewish boyfriend cringed when I bought a book
By Nietzsche; I guess he thought that I could be
Seduced by anyone. Days blazed a blue
Streak over the mountains, San Miguel, sagebrush,
The one dormitory for female students.
I broke up with my boyfriend. I liked to walk alone
At night, under the moon, that other desert.

(Socorro)

NOSTALGIA OF THE INFINITE

With longing at once painful and pleasurable,
The Infinite recalls particulars
Of the past, the tints and textures of events:
Early light disclosing a vast savannah;
Later, the fallen columns of a Greek temple,
And later still, da Vinci in his studio.
Such knowledge is invigorating but
Burdensome, too. The Infinite labors under
A weight that would weigh it down were it anything
Less than infinite. The responsibility
Of the Infinite is to remember all that ever
Occurred, the sequencing that finally led
To itself. Pity the Infinite, for time
Is overwhelmingly long and issues in
More moments than infinity can count.

OLD AGE IN ENGLAND

A house, small and pretty, on a deadend road
In England. An easy train to Cambridge to
Play string quartets, a fast train to London
And cab ride to concerts. Five years like that,
With shared excitement and hilarious jokes.
Then one endures a stroke and the other
Develops dementia and now the small, pretty
House is too close, with triple-pane windows
That bottle up the corrosive stink of medicine
And through which the boxwood hedge can be seen
Approaching, like Birnam Wood to Dunsinane.
Grotesquerie now rules, the one frightened
By the other—how can she be married to
A man too stupid to think?—and the other
Fearing she will order him out of the house.
Where will he go? He tries to figure out
How much money he will have to live on
But he can't remember how to add zero
To zero. Desperate to flee each other,
They occupy silent, separate bedrooms.
There was a drought, then a rainy spell
During which poplars shed rain from yellow leaves,
Sixty-fourth notes slipping from forgotten staves.

PALM TREE

The trunk seems more homemade than grown,
The bark in stacks like building blocks.
These stacks tilt every which way and yet
Are firmly lodged and hold and hold up,
The branches leafy with fronds that sway
Like Hula dancers, with southern winds.
An odd tree, the palm tree, but cast
Against a sky, its curving blades
Suggest a refreshing shade. Against
The sea, the palm accentuates
The horizontal line, the pale
Azalea of the setting sun, cowlick
Of white cloud lost and floating in
The light blue over the darkening blue sea.

(Bahamas)

PARISIAN SKYSCAPE

Somehow like tulips, but solider than tulips,
The roofs of Paris compose blocks of color
As they do in paintings by Maurice de Vlaminck,
Resulting in a tender, cheerful skyscape
All angles and angels and gargoyles and belltowers.
In bistros, *les chefs* suavely serve *pommes frites*.
In boutiques, *les femmes chic* test-spray scents
By Cacherel, Chanel, Dior, Fragonard
On neatly turned wrists, and in *Les Halles*
Working men carry and carve and push and pull
And lift and throw down. An aerial view
Of the city of light discovers a circus of shadows,
Corners of darkness breaking the city into planes
That ask an artist to reassemble the whole.

QUESTION

This day, spread

Before us

Like honey

On bread.

Will you not eat?

SLOVENIA

Across the river came the sound:
Hiccupping outboard motor running
The jerrybuilt ferry to ground.

The ferry hove into view:
Two men and a car-wide raft.
Nothing under the sun is new

Except the old, and here we were,
Waiting to cross the river to
The Moravian Czech Republic, where

We planned to see the October moon
Shine above the castle in Prague.
The ferry clacked, the ferry boomed

Across the river. On the now-far side
Someone else now awaited.
We got in the car; we'd a long ride

Ahead of us still to cover the ground
Between the Nineteenth and Twenty-first Centuries.
The castle wore the moon as a crown.

SPARROW WITH PERSONALITY

Out of rosemary he leapt
And sauntered to our feet
Where we rested on a bench
Overlooking the lake
While whitecaps sported in
The wind. He came closer,
Tilting his head, so we
Could see the soft fuzz
On his face, as if he were
A teenage boy. He was
Not frightened—though, again
Like a teenage boy, he would
Not let us pick him up.
Now we look for him
In bush or branches, in air
Or on the lawn bordered
By blooms as glossy as
If a gardener slicked
Petals with Brilliantine.

(Bellagio)

TAORMINA

The quiet sea abided, the sun was strong.
Pines rushed down the hillside, a throng
Of them, whispering about the crazy birds in their hair.
A bird flew out to eat a pear dropped in an orchard.
A strange scene it was, the houses beneath palms,
The sea unearthly green. The pear was fly-specked,
The orchard drowsing. The sun stayed long,
A golden ring of light, then sank out of sight.

TOKYO

How do they do it, the Japanese?
Hotel rooms smaller than a shoe,
Steaks that cost a ransom, and
Hordes of runners that run over you
If you forget to look all ways
At once. And yet they know precisely how to
Sleep in beds half their size
(Or on mats on unforgiving floors)
And succeed at almost any enterprise.
A few dried reeds, a slatted blind
And everything is elegant.
It must be smarts, inborn intelligence
That sees them through their crowded lives.
Americans, surrounded by so much space,
Get lost, like keys and ballpoint pens, become
The clutter in the cluttered American home.

WEST TO BELLINGHAM

My future veered off course. Without direction,
Without a home, without lover or friend,
I traveled west as far as I could go.
The hills of Bellingham in Washington
Require negotiation, so steep are they,
Climbing faster than one's blood pressure
And leaving one to stop short and sigh,
Dizzied by a view of the bay, so blue,
And white with crowds of clouds that show no sign
Of rain. But rain it does, almost daily,
Though usually not for long, and then the sun
Returns to bless the sea, baptize the sky—
Rhetorical description, overblown
And falsely theological and yet
Is there not a kind of homely saintliness
In this middling "City of Subdued Excitement,"
(As Bellingham modestly advertizes itself),
In sun and water, salt air and sandy sidewalk,
The San Juan Islands penciled on the horizon,
And not to mention the small, furry dog
Ecstatically alive? My terrier
And I together toured the bayfront day
By day and side by side and step by step.

WHEN POLAR BEARS HAVE GONE

When polar bears have gone, the tear their leaving
Rent in the fabric of the world will close
Seamlessly, and the world will seem as full
As ever, as complete, as detailed
As before, just a little dingier,
The Arctic Circle fractionally less bright.

There will be nights when something warm and white
Lumbers through the room, its shadow cast
Upon the wall by pallid, waning moonlight,
Its hulk a moving ship, its shoulders straining,
A feather of fur floating to the floor,
And we shall wake and wonder at the strength

Of such a mighty beast and hear the heart
That beats within like nothing that has been.

WOMEN WRITERS VISIT THE CAVE OF THE MOUNDS IN WISCONSIN

Too dark to see one's hand before one's face
Too dark to see any part of oneself

A silence so final we were afraid to speak,

The five of us accustomed to speaking freely,
Accustomed to shaping language into art,

Jolted mute by our corporeal knowledge,
Now and new, of the grave, crypt, catacomb,

The tomb and time and generations gone
As thoroughly as if they never existed,

Of helplessness before the fact of death,
The pit flat black, the surrounding black as dense

As a dead man's brain.

The guide turned on a light and we were back
In the world but it was no longer the same world.

It was clear now how foolish were our ambitions
And how necessary to our survival.

YARD ART IN GEORGIA (U.S.)

Their presence was sudden.
A two-lane highway—
And there they were,
Life-size wood
Cutouts of people.
Or cardboard?

Faces and clothes
Painted on. A woman
Wearing a frown, a man
In overalls, children,
A dog or two,
A cat or three.

Standing close to the fence
And farther up the road,
On the other side, more,
standing; more, silent. Huddled
Together, as if
To meet the enemy,
Though not yet belligerent, just
Cautious. Waiting.

I felt a prickle on the back of my neck.
I realized my teeth were clenched.

Back on the first side, a third group
Flourishing shovels and rakes.
The curious children were as wary
As their parents, who
Were whispering, most of them—*a sound like hissing.*
A blue sky made the horror more intense
As they ran after us, throwing
Their shovels, waving
Their sharp-toothed rakes.

XANTIPPE

A scold, we're told. Fishwife. Ball-busting bitch.
Her name the definition of a shrew.

But a man who disses his wife reveals himself
An untrustworthy judge of character.

Socrates lingered in Athenian cafés,
Retsina and cheese curd on shady patios,
Conversing with pupils who refused to go home.
What could they learn at home, where youth were
Expected to be seen, not heard? The waiters
Brought figs and olives and bread and the region's wines.

A husband like that needs a strong hand and guidance.
He might be plug-ugly, but Xantippe knew
He was smart. So was she, earning most of the drachmas.

A good wife keeps honest accounts, trims the fat
From her husband's meat, and doesn't let him sleep too late.

Socrates appreciated a dash of spunk
In a wife. He probably called her his sweet, sugared lemon.
Sugar tit may have been his favorite endearment.

If it is true that she once poured the contents of their chamberpot
Over her husband's head, he likely deserved it.

ZINNIA

The zinnia is a flower a child can grow.
At ten I planted a whole, short row
Of zinnias next to our rented house on a farm
Called Brookbury, unless, as my sister says,

The spelling was Brookberry. My brother said
The place was ugly, dull, prefabricated,
But I remember a balcony off my room,
Two staircases, a tilled field, and my room

Had five walls. Or maybe not, but so
It seemed to me. There's no way now to know
The truth of over sixty years ago,
No way to collate conflicting memories

Nor do I know the colors of the blooms
I tended, thinking of the flowerless rooms
That I would brighten with colorful bouquets
Of mildest sunlight and setting crimson rays.

New Poems

WHO WE ARE

Most of us want to think of ourselves as kind.
        At least within limits, limits being ticks and fruit flies,
        employers who pay less than fifteen dollars an hour,
        the racist, the ignorant president,
the friend who moved to California
and promptly forgot you. Failed to include your work
in his well-known anthology. Now you get
it, that he was never going to include you.
Still, we dislike ourselves for the grievances
that ooze from our mouths when we meant to be
civilized and forgiving. He was too busy,
you tell yourself, I tell myself, plenty
of people tell themselves: had more on his hands than anyone
could handle. So cut him some slack. Just don't imagine
he's ever going to get in touch with you
again.   Now, the question is how to set
such grievances aside and remember that
precisely because you have felt pain you must
be kinder than ever. Believe it or not, the world
without kindness is the death of hope. Someone
reaches out for help, and if you turn away
you find yourself on the bottom of the ocean,
drowning or drowned, no longer able to breathe.
We must help one another to breathe. We owe that.
Underwater, life turns dark and darker,
pressure may cause us to explode just like
a bomb on the streets of sad, bombarded Aleppo.
We are fallible and fragile, creatures
in need of air, warmth, solid ground, and company.
There were five birds on the same block of suet
at the feeder this morning. If they can get along,
why can't we? Of course, life is rarely simple.
There are unnamed roads, sinkholes, washed-out bridges,
out-of-date directional gadgets, and motels
in which you hope never to end up.
And yet the day is mild and energizing
and you find yourself singing in spite of yourself,
leaves like a tent over your head, a canopy
like the four-poster bed you look forward to sleeping in
with your spouse when you arrive home at end of day,
glad to be alive, glad to be where
you are now.

GETTING THERE

        And so it happens: one day you reach your goal.
        Are you happy? Disbelieving? Do others agree
        that you have reached your goal? Maybe not.
        Maybe no one sees the difference
in you or what you have done.
There's no celebration, no cake or ice cream.
You have something on your mind but no one
is interested. Guess what: you are not the center
of anything. Everybody is filled
to overflowing with himself or herself.
Each of us is centered in ourselves
but none of us are part of anyone else.
We are like lemmings who, instead of jumping
off a ledge together, jump one by one, sailing
into the sea. But don't try this unless
you know how to swim. Butterfly,
back stroke, crawl, side stroke, breaststroke, free style—
any of these will do. You may also
swim underwater or snorkel with flat fish.
I suppose I sound like a grouch but only because
grouching, more often than not, is how we tell
the truth. Although I do recall how it felt
to do what I did, and how elated and excited
I was to have done what I did, which had nothing
to do with swimming or fishing. Rather, it had
to do with me, just me, me myself
and I as we used to say in school, although
I have no idea now why we said it.
Have you begun to see how cluttered, how
loosely all things connect with everything?
It's a problem, I tell you, storing so much data
in one's mind, and then there are the books,
the millions on millions of books you try
to retain but as soon as you finish just one,
you've forgotten how it began and begin
to question the end because even the end
is hard to remember as soon as you decide
to remember. Why is that? Maybe Pepsi
and Coca-Cola are eradicating
our aging noggins. We might instead meld
our brains into one Very Large Intelligent Brain

or Giant Algorithm but we know
already that would never work: We'd be
arguing with ourselves all day long,
confused and angry and then melancholy
because we are burned out yet nothing makes
sense. In fact, sense is what we want, Good
sense. So where do we go to find good sense?
Some would say the Bible. Others might
say in the world of science, which, after all
is self-correcting. Then there are the Crazies
who turn up all over the world, not to mention
the kooks, the cuckoos, the flaky, the unhinged,
the screwy, the touched, the schizoid, the psychos,
the lunatic, the batty, the mental, berserkers,
all of them mad as hatters and alarmed
by being late for—for what? Dinner.
Dinner's fine. Dinner's great. However,
for one who's starving, dinner is necessary
so let's do our best to feed the hungry, cheer
the despondent, give a dollar to one
in need of a dollar, teach the young, see
that every family has a clean and safe home,
look after the sick, especially the sick
children, and make someone laugh, because
laughter is the most important thing of all.

MY MOTHER AND STEWART GRANGER

When I was very little, I had a rocking chair.
One day I got angry and tried to throw
the rocking chair into the fire. Why we had
a fire in Louisiana I do not know.
Anyway, I got too close to the fire
and burned a scar into my neck and upper chest.
I don't remember doing this, but the scar
is proof that I did. Why was I angry?
Our parents were never around. My father
loved my little sister more than me.
My brother sometimes paid attention to me
but sometimes not. By the time we moved
to Ithaca, he was hanging out a lot
with bad guys, stealing cars and drinking,
wanting to marry his fifteen-year-old girlfriend.
No one knew what to do with him. No one
knew what to do with me. Our little sister
sat crying on the floor in the bedroom while
my brother grabbed me by my arm and slung
me around and around as if he wanted
to send me flying into hell. If
he had let go of me, I would have broken
into two. That did not happen, but
our mother was so mad that she would not
go to the movie they had planned to see
(she had a crush on Stewart Granger and
wanted to see *King Solomon's Mines*.) She swore
right then she would never again go
to a movie, to any movie anywhere
that night or any other. She retreated
into her room and never saw another
as if that would change something, but
nothing ever changed.

ROSES IN RUSSIA

You were in another country, and that country
was riddled with rules and regulations, spies
following you in a car simply because
you were an American. That was a lifetime
ago but you still remember the telephone
ringing at midnight to say your friend was dead.
For a moment you believed it. But the phone
rang again and again, thereby convincing you
that it wasn't true. And it was not true.
What a strange country, Russia, and now a crooked
country, oligarchs getting and spending while
the honest poor live like groundhogs, under-
ground, on cheap vodka and soothing borsht
and bread, waiting for freedom to find them.
There are those who've tried but, remarkably,
they always end up in prison, minds and hearts
wasting, rose petals dropping one by one.

ELSEWHERE

> Italic lines are by Dan O'Brien, from his poem
> "The Poet in Afghanistan," in his book *New Life: Poems*

Elsewhere in the meantime, O'Brien says,
we'll find our new story. So we travel
all the way to elsewhere and fail to find
our new story. Or my own new story.
Or yours. Indeed, we begin to think there is
no new story anywhere. We've used up
all the plots and characters, beginnings and ends.
We'd go elsewhere had we not already done so.
But look, a miniscule ant has climbed the length
of my pen and is now on the page. I do not wish
to kill it so I shake the page until the ant falls off.
It too is now elsewhere. In the meantime,
I'll write a poem.

CONTRA RILKE

> *You must change your life.*
> —Rainer Maria Rilke

For the most part it is not necessary to change your life.
Life will change your life without your help or permission.
You may want to plan for this or that,
but recognize that plans may go astray.
Should you still want to change your life,
imagine how it will be. Is that you
in a negligee awaiting a lover?
Is that you in jeans and sweater,
missing your family? When your family left,
that changed things, didn't it? Changed them big time,
probably far more than Rilke expected.
We are accidents of history,
and history is forever.

THESE TALL TREES

Like straws in soda, these tall trees bend,
forcing the grass to fall forward.
Time is the jewel in the peacock's train of hidden feathers.
Death travels with the wind.

WILD FLOWER

It finds a way when there is no way,
emerges despite its shyness.
A wild flower is determined to play.

On this windy, flashing day, we watch it wave.
Yet not for long are the pretty petals displayed.
This fact hushes us: flowers are brave.

BLOSSOMS DANCING

A breeze in May's as gentle as a doctor
treating a child. It will do no harm,
will only lightly alight upon a petal
here or there. Is it blue, pink, or yellow?
Or white, that color or non-color so
often connected with death or rebirth?
Nevermind. The flower itself says nothing
about the meaning of a single bloom.
It rejoices in its short life, and when
it dies, considers death a homecoming.

A WRITER AND HER COMPUTER

She lives with it. Loves it so much sometimes
she sleeps with it. Her lover, she thinks, ruefully
remembering romantic days of yore.
But who else can write her poems? Not that plenty
of people are not writing their own poems,
formal or free, written, we'd thought, with words
but now the words are redacted or
plunked in a circle or some other clever
innovation by some other poet.
Yet she persists, altogether happy
to write in the olden way, even as
computers evolve, someday to park themselves
inside our brains, making us smarter than ever
though possibly slightly a little less poetic.

HUSBAND WITH BOOK

       Wherever he goes, he has one with him: a book,
       I mean. Some are great books, some trivial,
       although he argues for the merits of
       thrillers and detective stories, mystery
       novels, almost anything with words.
       He also adores history and science.
       Speaking as a wife, I have to say
       it is not easy to keep up with him.
       Or rather, I simply should not be in this poem.
       The duet consists of my husband and
his book, whichever book it may be.
I peek into his room—he's reading—I know
not what—then sneak out, silent as a doe.

WAR AND PEACE

Likely the best title a writer has come
up with. War and peace are always in play.
War interrupts peace, leaving us dead or maimed
or simply missing. Peace does not so much
interrupt as intervene. In either case,
they brush against each other, the space between
less than what we'd like to see. We'd like
to see them billions of miles apart, with peace
being where we are and war far off and willing to cease.

BREAD AND BUTTER

A restaurant in our neighborhood
bakes the best bread I have tasted.
Ever. The best bread ever. I could eat
this bread for breakfast, lunch, and dinner, with

breaks for more bread. Equally, the butter,
sinking into the bread, makes the diner
salivate. Mmm Mmm good,
we say by way of thanking the heroic baker.
Mmm Mmm good, we say by way of congrat-
(insert chewing here), ulating ourselves
for patronizing this restaurant. Mmm Mmm
good, we say, thanking bakers everywhere.

HARRIET TUBMAN AND THE UNDERGROUND RAILWAY

Harriet ran the Underground Railway,
sending slaves northward. That took courage and
calculation. She was expert at both,
saving those who would otherwise be hanged
from a noose or burnt alive or fatally shot.
No, there was no physical railroad: she sent
them to houses she knew would take them in,
that is, safehouses. She organized and led
a sortie in war, spied for the Northern states,
and found men who'd fight for John Brown.
She had the good sense to buy a property
and there looked after her ageing parents.
Later she stood up as a suffragette.
Whatever she looked like, she was beautiful.

FORK AND KNIFE

They gaze at each other until the plate intervenes.
In America, the fork goes on
the left while in Europe it goes on the right.
Either way, each dreams of the other.
The quiet fork wants to join her lover,
to be held tightly by the handsome, powerful knife
that could break her in two but for one of life's
little mysteries: that the strongest man
willingly concedes to the weakest woman.

THE SKY AND THE STARS

To repeat: We love to watch the sky
when stars are on show. How lovely is this pairing,
the greatest show on earth though it is not
on earth. Nor would we say elephants
and tigers are on display. May elephants
and tigers enjoy their lives on safe grounds
and obtain a good night's sleep while we
gaze at the lights overhead, bemused
with thoughts of time and space and distances
impossible to grasp. Is there an edge
where time meets the end? Or a ledge
upon which distance turns back on itself like
the snake who swallows its tail? Mystery
is what we see when we look into the sky,
and the uncountable plenty of blossoming stars.

Cover artist Dawn Surratt studied art at the University of North Carolina at Greensboro as a recipient of the Spencer Love Scholarship in Fine Art. She has exhibited her work throughout the Southeast and currently works as a freelance designer and artist. Her work has been published internationally in magazines, on book covers, and in print media. She lives on the beautiful Kerr Lake in northern North Carolina with her husband, one demanding cat, and a crazy Pembroke Welsh Corgi.

Kelly Cherry is the former Poet Laureate of Virginia (2010–2012) and is the author of twenty-six books, ten chapbooks, and two translations of classical drama. She is an Emeritus Member of Poets Corner at the Cathedral Church of St. John the Divine in New York City, and was the first recipient of the Hanes Poetry Prize from the Fellowship of Southern Writers. Her many other awards include fellowships from the National Endowment for the Arts and the Rockefeller Foundation, a Bradley Achievement Award, the William "Singing Billy" Walker Award for Lifetime Achievement in Southern Letters, the L.E. Phillabaum Poetry Award, the Carole Weinstein Prize in Poetry, and a USIS Speaker Award (the Philippines). She is the Eudora Welty Professor Emerita of English and Evjue-Bascom Professor Emerita in the Humanities, University of Wisconsin Madison, and a University of Alabama in Huntsville Eminent Scholar, 2001–2005. She and her husband live on a farm in Virginia.

www.ingramcontent.com/pod-product-compliance
Lightning Source LLC
Chambersburg PA
CBHW020051170426
43199CB00009B/249